THE BLACK BEAR

OTHER TITLES AVAILABLE THROUGH CONVERPAGE:

0-9728155-0-3 America Illustrated
0-9728155-1-1 The Biography of a Grizzly
0-9728155-5-4 My RV A User's Guide
0-9728155-6-2 The Maritime History of Massachusetts 1783-1860
0-9728155-7-0 And Illustrated Treatise on the Art of Shooting
0-9728155-9-7 The Runaway Deer
0-9815720-0-6 A Little Dusky Hero
0-9815720-1-4 The Black Bear

Visit www.converpagestore.com for details and pricing. Watch our library grow!

CONVERPAGE SPECIALIZES IN THE REPRODUCTION OF
RARE AND OUT-OF-PRINT BOOKS

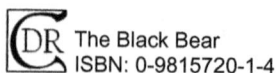

The Black Bear
ISBN: 0-9815720-1-4
Digitally reproduced in 2008 by:
Converpage - Digital Reproductions
23 Acorn Street, Scituate, MA 02066
www.converpage.com

Ben and the author

THE BLACK BEAR

BY

WILLIAM H. WRIGHT
Author of "The Grizzly Bear"

ILLUSTRATED FROM PHOTOGRAPHS BY THE AUTHOR
AND J. B. KERFOOT

CHARLES SCRIBNER'S SONS
NEW YORK - - - - 1910

CONTENTS

ILLUSTRATIONS

THE STORY OF BEN

THE STORY OF BEN

My story of Ben starts on the 22d of June, 1890. Ben's own story had begun some four or five months earlier, in the den where his mother, who was a Black Bear, had spent the winter; but although I came to know Ben rather intimately later on, he never spoke of his early childhood to me and I never asked him about it. So we'll take that part for granted.

Early in May of that year three of us, Martin Spencer, Jack O'Brien, and myself, had set out from Spokane, Washington, to hunt grizzlies and prospect for gold in the rugged and, at that time, largely unexplored Bitter Root Mountains, in Idaho. We had a small pack train and a large stock of enthusiasm, and we arrived at the foothills with both in good condition. But although it was well past the middle of the month when we reached the mountains, we soon found ourselves floundering in snow-drifts that increased in depth as we climbed, and when, for several days on end, we had cut our way with a two-handed saw through fallen trees that barred our progress and had dug the saddle and pack horses out of pot holes in the snow into which a misstep or an act of deliberate stupidity had sent them rolling, both men and horses had become exhausted. And so, when a cold storm had added itself to our other troubles, we had pitched camp in a little opening facing the south and settled down to wait for better days. And we had waited there three solid weeks.

Once, on the morning of the 19th of June, dawn had shown us a clear sky, against which, fifty miles to the east of us, we could see the main range of the jagged Bitter Roots; and after eating a cheerful breakfast we had hastily broken camp, packed our horses, and started for the summit of the ridge along which we proposed to travel. But here, roaring up out of the next valley, we had met another great storm of icy wind and swirling snow, and I had soon been forced to leave my companions with the horses while I stumbled down the mountain and hunted up another sheltered spot where we could take refuge from the huge storm. And so by noon we had once more found ourselves crowded under a hemlock bark lean-to, thankfully facing a blazing fire of logs and listening to the wind howling overhead. And it was not until the afternoon of the 21st that the storm had passed. Then at last the sun had come out hot and clear and had begun forcing the great masses of snow that clung to the limbs of the trees to loosen their grip so that the forest was filled with the splash of their falling, while laden bushes jerked their heads free from the weight that bore them down and the horses stood steaming with the warm air.

But the burnt child fears the fire, and we had determined to be dead sure of the weather conditions this time before we went ahead; so we first climbed to the top of the ridge to study the country through our glasses and at the same time try to look a little bit into the future in the matter of the weather. The storm, we found, covered a tract of country about fifteen miles in width and fifty to sixty miles in length, and where we stood was about midway of the western end of its range. Some two miles along the ridge on which we were we could see a gap in the hills, and Spencer and I started over to explore this, while Jack took his rifle and a dog that he had brought along and started down the mountain.

Spencer and I, after reconnoitring the gap, catching a mess of small trout from a stream that flowed through it, and following the track of a large grizzly for some miles, reached camp after dark, and found that O'Brien had returned some time before after having had a more interesting adventure. It seemed that, when some two miles from camp, he had heard, above the constant splash of falling snow, the crying of some animals, and as the sound seemed to be coming nearer and nearer he had crouched down behind a large log and, holding his dog in check, had waited and watched. Shortly, out from among the trees, there appeared a large Black Bear followed by three tiny cubs, the whole family having evidently just left their winter quarters.

It must have been an amusing procession, for the old bear was ploughing her way through the soft and slushy snow, making large holes into which the baby bears would fall, and out of which, being so small, they were scarcely able to flounder. They were quite unable, therefore, to keep the pace set by their mother, and the old bear would slouch along for a while and then sit down and watch them as they struggled to catch up. And all the time they kept up the whimpering, crying sound that had attracted Jack's attention.

But I am afraid O'Brien was more interested in bear meat than in bear habits, for as soon as these animals drew near his hiding-place he let loose the dog, who drove the mother up one tree and the cubs up another; and having shot the old one and decided that it might be possible to catch the youngsters alive next day, he returned to camp.

The next morning, as soon as we had had breakfast, we put pack saddles on a couple of ponies and, taking some empty gunny-sacks along in which to put the cubs if we caught them, started out to bring in the meat and hide of the old bear. It had come on to rain again during the night, and a cold drizzle was falling as we started out; and in that steep-sided and unbroken wilderness, half buried in the melting snows of a mountain winter, the going was both slow and dangerous. However, we managed to reach the bottom of the ravine where Jack had seen the bears without accident, and once near the place we tied the horses and crept forward as silently as might be, thinking to steal up on the cubs unheard and perhaps catch them before they could reach and climb a tree. The carcass of the dead bear lay about fifty feet from a huge fir tree, and we soon saw the three cubs, huddled together, and sitting on the body of their dead mother. But it was evident that they were aware of our approach, for they were on the alert and keeping a sharp lookout in our direction. So when we had worked up as near as possible, and had reached the last cover between ourselves and them, we crouched behind a fallen log and laid out a plan of campaign.

It was plain to be seen that we were not going to catch the cubs off their guard, and it was equally evident that we would have to do some mighty quick sprinting if we were going to beat them to the foot of the big fir tree. So we agreed to move forward little by little until the bears began to be alarmed, and then to make a dash for the tree in hope of intercepting them. But we had scarcely wormed our way over the log and begun our sneaking approach, when all three cubs rose on their hind legs for a clearer view of their suspicious visitors, and a moment later they bounded down from their bed in the dead mother's fur and began floundering through the snow and water toward the fir tree.

The little fellows (the largest of them would not have

weighed over five pounds) had looked to be half dead with cold and misery, and the snow and slush was over their heads; but for all that they reached the tree ahead of us, and started up the rough trunk like so many cats. I just managed to grab the hindmost of them by one leg as she was scrambling out of reach, and after a good deal of squalling, clawing, and biting, the little woolly ball was landed in one of the gunny-sacks, the mouth tied up, and the package deposited on a log out of the way. Then we began figuring out ways and means of catching the two cubs in the big fir tree. The rough trunk of this old settler shot up forty feet from the ground without a limb, and the cubs looked down at us from the lowest branches, pushing out their upper lips and uttering short "whoofs," exactly as a grown bear would have done. There seemed to be but one way to get them alive, and this was to shin up the old tree and shake them down as one would ripe plums. Spencer and Jack agreed to catch them before they could again take to a tree, if I would undertake the climbing and shaking: and after some little talk I closed the bargain. The hardest part of the task seemed to me to be the shinning of the old tree. The rest looked easy, but that was before I had tried it. Any one who has never had the pleasure of dislodging a bear from the limb of a tree by shaking is apt to think it an easy matter; but he will change his mind after a little experience.

The bark of the fir tree was rough and afforded good finger holds, and it also scraped the skin off the inside of my knee, but in due time I reached the lower limbs and, seating myself on one of these, rested for a few minutes. Then I began climbing up after the cubs, who moved higher up at my approach. One of them, after climbing some twenty feet, crawled out on a branch and, as I came to him first, I gave the limb a gentle shake expecting to see him roll off and go tumbling down through the boughs to the ground below. As the cub did not drop at the first shake, I gave another and harder one. As this did not dislodge him, I stood on the branch and, grasping the limb over my head with both hands jumped up and down with all my might and, after several minutes of this exercise, saw the youngster lose his desperate grip on the small branches and go smashing down out of sight. And a moment later a loud splash announced his arrival at his destination. Even then, I learned afterward, he got to his feet and had nearly reached another tree before he was captured.

The racket that had been raised in dislodging the one cub had so frightened the other that he had climbed to the topmost branch of the tree, and here I found him with his head down, snorting and striking with his little paws. If he had weighed fifty pounds he would have been an ugly customer to handle, but as it was there was no danger from him. But there was considerable difficulty, for he had climbed so high that I did not dare trust my weight to the small branches, and, shake as I might, I was unable to dislodge him. Finally I climbed down to where the limbs were longer, cut one of them with my jack-knife, and, using it as a pole, succeeded in poking the cub out of his perch. And as he shot past me I called to the boys to look out and listen for the splash of his arrival. But instead of the expected sound I heard Martin call out that the cub had caught on a lower limb and was climbing back up the tree. This was aggravating, but I thought that at least I had the upper hand of him this time and started down to meet him.

He had taken refuge on one of the longest branches of the old fir, and as he was too far out for me to reach with my pole, I had recourse to my former tactics. I stood up on the branch the cub was on, grasped a higher one with both hands, and put all my strength and weight into a succession of violent shakes. The bear slipped inch by inch out toward the end of the limb; first one paw and then the other lost its grip; at last he hung down from the outermost fork by what looked like one toe nail. But further than this he refused to yield. Round and round he swung as long as the shaking lasted, which was until I was completely out of wind and compelled to stop for breath; and then back the little beggar climbed, and by the time I had got ready for another inning he was safe in the original position.

This was repeated again and again until it became evident that only complete exhaustion on the part of one or other of the contestants would end the bout. And I won by a hair. The plucky little fellow let go and was landed squalling in the sack with the others, while I rested up before undertaking my slower journey to the ground. Then we skinned the old bear, cut up the meat, packed the whole on the horses, fastened the sack containing the cubs to one of the packs, and returned to camp.

Just back of the bark shack which we had built there was a steep bank, and into this, with pick and shovel, we dug a hole. Over the top of the excavation we placed poles, and having covered these with bark threw a foot or more of dirt on top, thus making a nice little cave for the cubs. We then gathered pine needles, dried and warmed them by the fire, and filled up the den with them. From a tanned buckskin we cut long thongs, fastened little buckskin collars around our orphans' necks, and so tied them to a stake driven into the ground in front of the cave. We each, naturally, laid claim to a cub. And as I was given first choice as a reward for the climbing I had done to get them, I chose the determined, spunky little chap that had been the last one caught. He was the middle one in size, but I made up my mind to treat him gently and keep him, if possible, until he should be a large bear. Jack took the first one caught, it being the smallest

and a female. The other two were males. Spencer
named his bear George, Jack decided to bring his up
without any name, while I called my wee cublet Ben,
after "Ben Franklin," the pet grizzly of one of my
boyhood's heroes, old James Capen Adams, the tamer
and exhibitor of grizzly bears who, in the fifties and
sixties, became famous as Grizzly Adams.

But now that we had caught our cubs, housed them,
parcelled them out, and named them, we had to face
another problem. How were we going to feed them,
and, worse still, *what* were we going to feed them?
Old Grizzly Adams, when he caught his "Ben" as an
even tinier cub than mine, had induced a greyhound
that he had with him and that happened to have
puppies at the time to nurse the foundling. But
Jack's dog could not help us that way and we had to
make other arrangements.

We began by taking a frying-pan, a little flour and
water, some condensed milk and a pinch of sugar, and
stewing up a sort of pap. When this had cooled off
we each took a teaspoon and a squalling, kicking cub
and began experimenting. The cubs, small as they
were, had sharp claws, teeth like needles, and a violent
objection to being mollycoddled; and so, although we
each had on heavy buckskin gloves, and each held a
cub under one arm, its front paws with one hand and
a teaspoon with the other, the babies took most of their
first meal externally. The little rascals looked like pasty

polar bears when the fight was over. But they acted better the second try and soon learned to like their new diet. And in a day or two they learned to feed themselves out of a plate. And it was not very long before our problem was, not to induce them to eat, but to satisfy their unappeasable appetites.

Meanwhile, however, we had had other troubles. At the conclusion of their first meal we had put them into their den, placed sections of bark against the opening, rolled a boulder in front of the improvised door, and left them, as we thought, for the night. But we were soon awakened by the cries of the lonesome little fellows, and, as there seemed to be no prospect of their quieting down, I finally got up, built a fire, warmed some of the gruel, and gave them another feed. I then warmed a couple of flat rocks, placed these under the pine needles, and again tucked the babies into bed. By daybreak I had to get up and give them an early breakfast.

This was the first night, but it was no sample of what followed. The interval between feeds became less and less until the feeding quieted them only so long as the feeding act lasted. Then, as soon as a cub was put down, it set up a bawling that was unbearable. One night we put them all in a sack and tied the mouth. This kept them from bawling so long as they could not get out of the sack, but they all fell to work with tooth and nail, and their combined voices soon

announced that they had succeeded in freeing themselves and were pacing in front of their cave making
it impossible for us to sleep. I got up and put them
into another sack, and this sack inside another. Then
I put the bundle in the den and, with the shovel, buried
it more than a foot deep with dirt. Then I put rocks
over the top and front of their house. At first the
snuffing and snorting they made in working on the
sack was nearly as bad as the bawling, but we finally got
to sleep in spite of it; only, however, to be aroused
later on by familiar sounds that proclaimed that the
sacks had been clawed to bits, the cave dug open, and
that the trio were waiting to see what kind of game we
would next invent for their entertainment. This was
our last attempt to keep them quiet. After that we
fed them all they would eat and then let them howl.

During the day they would play contentedly in front
of the den for a part of the time. But when the two
male bears settled down to sleep the little vixen of a
female would howl and fret and finally take to clawing
and biting them, so that at last they would come out
and join in her walking and bawling. As soon as we
discovered this we separated them, making another
cave for the female, and after this we were not bothered
so much with the crying, and in a few days this ceased
altogether.

We stayed at this camp more than two weeks,
waiting for the weather to settle; and though we did

some fishing and a little hunting we were, for the most part, held close by the steady rain and gave much time to the training of our cubs. Each of us of course adopted his own system of education. O'Brien, being an Irishman, would hear of no half measures; talked of "sparing the rod and spoiling the child," and was determined to be master in his own house. In this way he soon developed a disposition in his little cub that I have never seen equalled for viciousness in any animal whatever. She would, at the mere sound of Jack's voice, become a vindictive little devil; and she would spit, and strike at, and fight him until she was completely exhausted. And when she finally died from the effects of the constant whippings he gave her in trying to break her spirit, she tried to bite him with her last breath.

Ben and George occupied the original little cave in the bank, and we spent many hours laughing at their antics. At first they would scratch and bite if you touched them, but we never whipped them nor corrected them in any way and they soon lost their fear of us. We put on heavy leather gloves, handled them gently but firmly, and—let them chew. They were so small that they could do us no harm and after a few days they grew gentle as kittens. It was not long before, when they were not tied up, they would come and climb into our laps. They would lick our hands like puppies and, when allowed to, would come into our tent and snuggle down beside us on our blankets. During the whole five years that I kept Ben I never once struck or whipped him and never allowed any one to tease him, and a more gentle and playful animal I never saw.

Just in front of their little den there was a large stump with a long root that sloped away down the bank. One day when Spencer was playing with the cubs, he picked up one of them and placing it, doubled up like a ball, on the old root, sent it rolling downward. To our amazement the bear did not try to regain his feet until he stopped rolling some fifteen feet away, and Spencer was so tickled with the act that he brought him back and once more sent him tumbling down the incline. The result was the same as before. The bear kept whirling until he landed at the end of the root. The other cub was now brought out and we found that he would do the same thing. We sent them down, first backward, then forward, and either way the little fellows seemed to enjoy the sport as much as we; and it was not long before they would climb up on the root and, ducking their tiny heads, would go rolling down the toboggan slide, and in the end we actually had to tie them up to keep them from overdoing it.

Sometimes they would play like kittens. They would roll over and over, biting and wrestling, and we would laugh until our sides fairly ached. At other times they seemed to feel cranky and out of sorts, and

Making friends

then they would claw and fight each other. These spells always occurred when they were tied to their stake and were pacing the circle in front of their cave.

We continued to keep them fastened most of the time by their buckskin leads to the stake driven near their den, and they spent much of their time walking round and round in circles. They never however, by any chance, accompanied each other in the same direction, but invariably travelled different ways; and for the most part they rather ignored each other when they met on these journeys, or stopped to play in all friendliness. Perhaps they would pass without noticing each other a dozen times, when suddenly, as they met again, they would rise on their hind legs and look at each other with an expression of complete surprise, as who should say: "Where in all creation did *you* come from? Here I have been travelling this circle for half an hour, and never mistrusted there was another bear in this part of the country." And then, as though determined to celebrate the lucky meeting, they would embrace and tumble about for a few minutes and then separate and, perhaps, pass each other a dozen times more with no notice taken. And then the little comedy would be re-enacted.

But on days when their tempers were touchy these meetings were apt to be less playful. Instead of surprise they would then exhibit resentment at finding their imaginary solitude invaded; and after a few

spiteful slaps with their little paws, they would clinch
and bite and claw each other in earnest. Usually they
would break away from these clinches quite suddenly
and resume their tramp; only, however, to reopen
hostilities at an early date. Ben, although the smaller
of the two, always seemed to get the better of his brother in the boxing bouts and wrestling matches. He entered into each with an earnestness that seemed to put
the larger cub to flight; and yet in spite of the fact that
as they grew older their battles seemed to grow more
fierce, we thought nothing of the matter, but looked on
and laughed at the Lilliputian struggles. But one day
when we returned to camp we found George dead in
the little trail that circled the stake to which they were
tied, while Ben in his rounds stepped over the body
of his dead brother at each turn. George's face and
nose were chewed beyond identification and he had
been dead several hours.

Ben had now no companions except ourselves and
one of the dogs which I had brought along and whose
name was Jim; but in spite of this, or because of it, he
grew more friendly and playful each day. He would
coax Jim to come and romp with him and they would
chase each other about until the dog was tired out.
Ben seemed to be tireless and would never quit playing until chained up, or until the badgered dog turned
on him in earnest. Even then the bear used not to
give up hope immediately. After the first really angry

snap from Jim, Ben would stand off a few feet and look apologetic. Then, if nothing more happened, he would approach the dog with a kind of experimental briskness; only, however, to turn a back somersault in his haste to get out of the reach of Jim's teeth. A few minutes later, after Jim had lain down and was apparently asleep, Ben would steal up quietly and, very gently, with just the tip of his paw, would touch his old play-fellow to find out if he really meant that the romp was off. And it was the deep growl that always greeted this last appeal that seemed to settle the matter in Ben's mind. He would then keep out of Jim's way until the latter felt like having another play.

Ben was very quick to learn and we only had to show him a few times to have him catch on to a new trick. He continued to enjoy cartwheeling down the old root, and one of the other things he took to with the most zest was a sort of juggling act with a ball. This trick, like the other, we discovered by accident, and then worked up into a more elaborate performance. We finally made him a large ball out of a length of rope, sewed it up in a gunny-sack to keep it from unwinding, and he would lie on his back and keep the thing spin-ning with his four feet by the hour.

Early in July the weather finally became settled. The new snow had melted away, the old snow banks were fast disappearing, the little open park on the side of the mountain above our camp was green with young grass and literally carpeted with flowers. So one morning we rounded up the ponies, saddled and packed them, put the cub into a grain sack, tied up the mouth, placed it on top of one of the packs, tied each of its four corners to one of the lash ropes that held the pack to the horse, and started into the unexplored Clearwater country in the heart of the Bitter Roots.

The horse selected for Ben's mount was a little tan-colored beast who gave very little trouble on the trail, and whom we called Buckskin. We never had to lead him and he would always follow without watching. He would, when he found good feed, loiter behind until the pack train was nearly out of sight; but then, with a loud neigh, he would come charging along, jumping logs and dashing through thick bushes until the train was again caught up with. The first day's travel was a dangerous one for the bear on account of the many low-hanging limbs. We were obliged to keep a constant watch lest one of these catch the sack and either sweep it from the pack or crush Ben to death inside it. But with care and good luck we got through safely and, after seven hours of travel, reaching an open side hill with plenty of feed for the horses and a clear cold spring, we went into camp.

While we were unpacking the horses an old trapper and prospector known as Old Jerry came along. He was one of the first men who made their way into that wilderness, and for many years he and his cabin on the

Lockasaw Fork of the Clearwater were among the curiosities of the region. We had put Ben, still in his sack, on the ground while we got things settled for the night, and Old Jerry, seeing the sack moving, asked what we had in it. When he heard that it was a Black Bear cub he asked permission to turn it out and have a look at it and we told him to go ahead. After loosening the cord that closed the mouth, he took the sack by the two lower corners and gave it a shake, and out rolled Ben in his favorite toboganning posture of a fluffy ball. The cub seemed to think this a variation of the pine root game, and to the astonishment and delight of Old Jerry continued turning somersaults for ten or fifteen feet. Old Jerry is still alive, and to this day I never meet him that he does not speak of my performing cub.

The next day we again put Ben in the sack, but this time we cut a hole in the side of it, so that he could ride with his head out. For a while he was contented with this style of riding, but after some days he got to working on the sack until he was able to crawl through the hole. Then, as we found that he could keep his seat very nicely and would even, when his pony passed under a branch or leaning tree, dodge to one side of the pack and hang there until the danger was past, we adopted his amendment and from this time on never again put him in the sack when on the march. Instead, we arranged to give him a good flat pack to ride on. We put a roll of blankets on each side of the horse, close up to the horns of the pack saddle, and tied them in place. Then the space between was filled with small articles and a heavy canvas thrown over all and cinched in place. And on top of this Ben would pass the day. We tied his lead to the lash rope and he seemed perfectly content, and in fact appeared to enjoy the excitement of being jolted and shaken along through the timber and brush. It kept him on the jump to dodge the limbs and switches that were always threatening to unseat him, but in all of his four months' riding through the mountains, I never saw him taken unawares. Nor was he ever thrown by a bucking horse. Sometimes he would get down from his seat on top of the pack and sit on the pony's neck, holding by one paw to the front of the pack. Sometimes he would lie curled up as though asleep. But he was never caught off his guard, and his horse Buckskin seemed not to care how much he climbed about on its back.

Ben soon came to know his own horse, and after Buckskin was packed of a morning would run to the pony's side and bawl to be lifted to his place on the pack. And once there he spent several minutes each morning inspecting the canvas and the ropes of his pack. Several times during the summer we were obliged to transfer Ben to another mount, but we had to be mighty careful in our arrangements, as we learned to our cost the first time we tried the experiment.

The next day we cut a hole in the sack so that he could ride
with his head out

This was on a day when we had a difficult mountain to descend, and we thought we would lighten Buckskin's load by putting Ben on another horse that was carrying less weight. We got him settled on Baldy, as we called the other cayuse, without any trouble, and started out in the usual order; but just as we were on a particularly steep part of the hill, working our way down through a track of burned but still standing timber where the dry dirt and ashes were several inches deep and the dust and heat almost unbearable, there was a sudden commotion in the rear. We turned to see what was happening, and out of a cloud of dust and ashes Baldy bore frantically down upon us. His back was arched and with his head down between his forelegs he was giving one of the most perfect exhibitions of the old-school style of bucking that any one ever saw.

Now it is useless to try to catch a bucking horse on a steep mountain side. The only thing to be done was to get out of the road and wait until the frightened animal either lost its footing and rolled to the foot of the declivity or reached the bottom right side up and stopped of its own accord. So we jumped to one side. But, just as Ben and his maddened steed enveloped in a cloud of ash dust swept past the balance of the now frightened horses, the pack hit against a dead tree whose root had nearly rotted away and the result completed the confusion. For the force of the shock first dislodged a large section of loosely hanging bark which came down with much noise, striking the head pack-horse squarely across the back; and this was almost instantly followed by the falling of the old tree itself, which came down with a crash of breaking limbs and dead branches, and sent up a cloud of dust that completely hid Ben and his cavorting mount as they tore down the mountain. This was too much for the leading pony, who already stood shivering with excitement, and turning sharp to the right he shot off around the side of the mountain.

The other horses were quickly tied up, and while Spencer hurried after the runaway leader I took down through the burned timber after Baldy. Had the latter known how hard it had been to shake that same little bear from the limb of the old tree, he never would have spent so much energy in trying to buck him off the top of the pack. Ben had not looked in the least troubled as he was hurried past us, but had apparently felt himself complete master of the situation. He had, however, almost instantly disappeared from view, and soon even the sound of the bounding pony and the breaking of the dead branches as the pack hit them was no longer to be heard. The only things that marked their course were the deep imprints of the pony's feet and the dust cloud that was settling down among the dead and blackened timber. Hurrying along this easily followed trail I at last reached the bottom of the gorge and found the tracks still leading up the opposite slope. But the horse had soon tired of the strenuous work of the steep ascent, and after a couple of hundred yards he had come to a standstill in a thick clump of trees and underbrush that had escaped the fire. Ben was still sitting in his place as unconcerned as though nothing had happened, but was liberally covered with ashes and did not seem to be in the best of humors. The pack did not appear to have slipped any and so I undid the lead rope and started back toward where the pack train had been left.

But when only a few yards on the way the pony suddenly bolted ahead, nearly knocking me down as he tried to get past. I brought him to a halt with a few sharp yanks on the rope, and then kept a careful eye to the rear to find out what it was that was startling him. I did not suspect Ben because none of the horses had ever shown the least fear of him, had always allowed him to run about them as they did the dogs, and no one of them had ever even kicked at him. Nevertheless I had noticed that the cub seemed grumpy when we put him on Baldy, and remembered that at first he had bawled and tried to get down. So I kept my eye on him. And the first thing I knew I saw him push out his upper lip, as all bears do when mad and out of humor, reach out stealthily one of his hind legs, and with a sharp stroke drive his catlike claws into Baldy's rump. So here was the cause of all the trouble.

Ben, objecting to the change of programme, had been taking it out on the horse. I at once tied him up so short that he could not reach the horse from the pack, and, although he was in a huff all that day, we had no further trouble with him. Only twice after this, however, did we mount him on any other horse but his own Buckskin.

Each day's travel now brought us nearer to the main range, and one day we climbed the last ridge and camped on the border of one of the beautiful summit meadows where grow the camas, the shooting-star, the dog-tooth violet, the spring beauty, and other plants that the grizzlies love. The snow, by now, had disappeared, except the immense banks lying in the deep ravines on the north side of the upper peaks; the marshes were literally cut up by the tracks of deer, elk, and moose; while freshly dug holes and the enormous tracks of grizzlies told us plainly that we had reached the happy hunting ground. And now I began to learn from Ben much about the wonderful instincts of animals. Ben had never, before we captured him, had a mouthful of any food except his mother's milk. Not only had the family just left the winter den in which the little cubs had been born, but the earth at that time, and for long after, had been covered deep with snow. So that there was nothing for even a grown bear to eat except some of the scant grasses that our horses found along the little open places on the sides of the hills, or the juices and soft slimy substances to be found beneath the bark of the mountain spruce trees in the spring and early summer.

But now, while camped near this mountain meadow, Ben would pull at his leash and even bawl to get loose, and I soon took to letting him go and to following him about to learn what it was that he wished to do. I was amazed to find that he knew every root and plant that the oldest bears knew of and fed upon in that particular range of mountains. He would work around by the hour, paying not the least attention to my presence; eat a bit of grass here, dig for a root there, and never once make a mistake. When he got something that I did not recognize, I would take it away from him and examine it to see what it was, and in this way I learned many kinds of roots that the bears feed on in their wild state. I have seen Ben dig a foot down into the ground and unearth a bulb that had not yet started to send out its shoot. Later, when the time came for the sarvis berries and huckleberries to ripen, he would go about pulling down bushes, searching for berries. And not once in the whole summer did I ever see him pull down a bush that was not a berry bush. This was the more remarkable because he would occasionally examine berry bushes on which there happened to be no berries at the time.

At our next camp we killed a small moose for meat, and the hide was used during the remainder of the trip as a cover for one of the packs. After a few days in the sun it dried as hard as a board and of course took the shape of the pack over which it had been used. And this skin box now became Ben's home when in camp. It was placed on the ground, Ben's picket pin driven near it, and he soon learned to raise up one edge and crawl inside. It was funny, when he had done some mischief in camp and we stamped our feet and took after him, to see him fly to the protection of his skin teepee, and raise the edge with one paw so quickly that there was no apparent pause in his flight. Then, safe inside, we would hear him strike the ground with his forefoot and utter angry "whoofs," daring us to come any nearer. After a few minutes the edge of the hide would be lifted a few inches and a little gray nose would peep out to see if the coast was clear. If no notice was taken of him he would come back into camp, only to get into trouble again and be once more shooed back to cover.

Ben took great pride in this home of his and was an exemplary housekeeper, for no insect was ever permitted to dwell in the coarse hair. At first, when the hide was green, the flies would crowd into the hair and "blow," or deposit their eggs. These Ben never allowed to hatch. As soon as he was off his pony he would get to work on his house, and with much sniffing and clawing, would dig out and eat every egg to be found. And not one ever escaped his keen little nose.

Many times in the night we would hear him sniffing and snuffing away, searching out the fly-blows.

He grew to be more of a pet each day and he still juggled his ball of rope. Indeed, he got to be a great expert at this trick. He knew his own frying-pan from the others, and would set up a hungry bawl as soon as it was brought out. His food in camp was still flour and water, a little sugar, and condensed milk. This we fed him for more than a month, after which we cut out the milk and gave him just flour and water with a pinch of sugar. He did not care about meat and would eat his frying-pan food, or bread, in preference to deer or moose meat. Sometimes, when we killed a grizzly, we would bring in some of the meat and cook it for the dogs. This was the only meat that Ben would touch and very little of that. But although he occasionally consented to dine on bear meat, he showed unmistakable signs of temper whenever a new bear-skin was added to our growing pile of pelts. On these occasions, even before the hide was brought to camp, we would find him on our return in a towering rage. No amount of coaxing would induce him to take a romp. Not even for his only four-footed friend, Jim, would he come out of his huff. He would retreat beneath his moose-skin house, and we could hear him strike the ground, champ his jaws, and utter his blowing "whoofs." I was never able to make out whether he resented or was made fearful by the killing of his kind, or whether it was the smell of the grizzlies, of which the Black Bear is more or less afraid, that affected him. He still remembered his mother, and on every occasion when he could get to our pile of bear hides he would dig out her skin—the only Black Bear skin in the lot—sniff it all over, and lie on it until dragged away. Indeed he seemed to mourn so much over it, even whimpering and howling every time the wind was in the right direction for him to smell it, that we finally had to keep this hide away from camp.

One day a little later on, as we were working our way toward the Montana side of the mountains, we arrived after a hard day's work at the bank of a large stream flowing into the middle fork of the Clearwater River. As the stream to be forded was a swift and dangerous one, and as we had as high a mountain to climb on the other side as the one we had come down, we decided to go into camp and wait till morning to find a practicable ford. In this deep canyon there was no feed for the horses, and not even enough level ground on which to set up our tent. So the horses were tied up to the trees, supper was cooked and eaten, Ben's "coop," as we called his skin house, was placed under a tree, and then each of us rolled up in his blankets and was soon lulled to sleep by the roar of the water over the boulders that lined the river's bed.

We were up and ready for the start before it was fairly light in the deep canyon, and, on account of

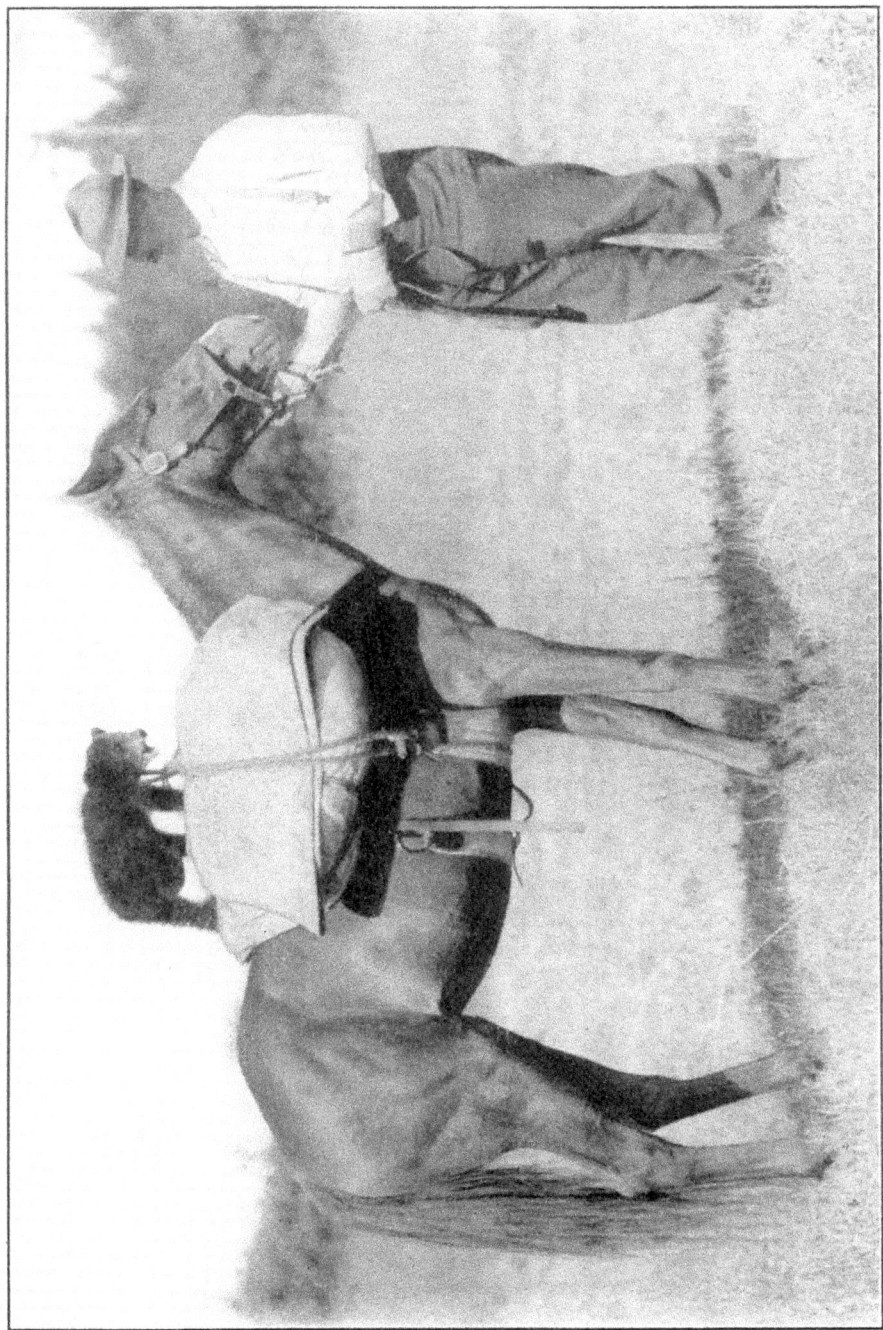

Ready for the start

the dangerous work ahead of us, both in fording the river and in climbing the opposite mountain, we determined to put Ben on a pony that could be led. We were careful, however, to tie him up short enough to prevent any repetition of his former antics. I then mounted my riding horse, a good sure-footed one, and, with the lead rope of Ben's horse in my hand, started for the other shore. The first two-thirds of the ford was not bad, but the last portion was deep and swift, the footing bad, and the going dangerous. However, by heading my horse diagonally down-stream, and thus going with the current, we succeeded in making the opposite bank in safety and waited for Spencer and Jack to follow. They got along equally well until near the bank on which I stood, when Spencer's horse slipped on one of the smooth rocks and pitched his rider over his head into the swirling water. With a pole which I had cut in case it should be needed I managed to pull the water-soaked fellow out of the current, however, and when we had seen once more to the security of the packs we started on the steep climb ahead of us. There was not so much as an old game trail to mark our way, and the hill was so steep that we could only make headway by what are known as "switchbacks." Our one desire now was to get up to where we could find grass for the horses, and a place level enough to pitch a tent and to unpack and give the ponies a few days in which to rest up.

The horse on which Ben had been mounted for the day was called Riley, and, as I have already said, we had selected him for his steady-going qualities and his reliability in leading. But just as we reached a particularly steep place about half-way up the mountain, Riley suddenly stopped and threw his weight back on the lead rope, which was lapped around the horn of my riding saddle, in such a way that the rope parted, the horse lost his balance, and falling backward landed, all four feet in the air, in a hole that had been left by an upturned root. We at once tied up the rest of the horses to prevent them from straying, and, cutting the cinch rope to Riley's pack, rolled him over and got him to his feet again. We then led him to as level a spot as we could find and once more cinched on the saddle, and, while Spencer brought the various articles that made up the pack, I repacked the horse. All this time nobody had thought of Ben. In the excitement of rescuing the fallen horse he had been completely forgotten, and when Spencer lifted the pack cover, which was the last article of the reversed pack, he called out in consternation, "Here's Ben, smashed as flat as a shingle." When we rushed to examine him we found that he still breathed, but that was about all; and after I got the horse packed I wrapped him in my coat, placed him in a sack, and hanging this to the horn of my riding saddle, proceeded up the hill.

In the course of a couple of hours we reached another of those ideal camping spots, a summit marsh, and here we unpacked the horses, turned them loose, set up our tent, and then looked Ben over to see if any bones were broken. His breathing seemed a little stronger, so I put him in the sun at the foot of a large tree and in a few minutes he staggered to his feet. We always carried a canful of sour dough to make bread with, and Ben was extravagantly fond of this repulsive mixture which he considered a dainty. I now offered him a spoonful of it, and as soon as the smell reached his nostrils he spruced up and began to lap it from the spoon; and from that time on his recovery was rapid. The next day he was as playful as ever and seemed none the worse for his close call.

Spencer had a great way, when we were about camp and Ben was not looking, of suddenly scuffling his feet on the ground and going "Whoof-whoof!" to frighten the cub. This would either send Ben flying up a tree or start him in a mad rush for his moose-skin house before he realized what the noise was. But one evening after this trick had been sprung on the cub several times, we came into camp well after dark, tired, hungry, and not thinking of Ben; and as Spencer passed a large tree there was a sudden and loud scuffling on the ground at his very heels and a couple of genuine "whoof-whoofs" that no one who had ever heard a bear could mistake. Spencer made a wild leap to one side and was well started on a second before he thought of Ben and realized that his pupil had learned a new trick and had incidentally evened things up with his master.

The acuteness of Ben's senses was almost beyond belief. Nothing ever succeeded in approaching our camp without his knowing it; and this not only before we could hear a sound ourselves, but before we could have expected even his sharp ears or sensitive nostrils to detect anything. He would stand on his hind feet and listen, or get behind a tree and peer out with one eye, and at such times nothing would distract his attention from the approaching object. Moreover whenever he had one of these spells of suspicion something invariably appeared. It might prove to be a moose or a deer or an elk, but something would always finally walk out into view. He was far and away the best look-out that I ever saw. We used to amuse ourselves by trying to surprise him on our return to camp; but, come in as quietly as we might, and up the wind at that, we would always find him standing behind a tree, peering around its trunk with just one eye exposed, ready to climb in case the danger proved sufficient to warrant it. One day after we had crossed the divide of the Bitter Root range into Montana, where we had gone to replenish our food supply before starting on our return trip, we camped in a canyon through which flowed an excellent trout stream. We were still miles from any settlement and had no idea that there was another human being in the same county. I was lying in the shade of a large tree with Ben, as his habit was, lying beside me with his head on my breast, to all appearance fast asleep. Suddenly he roused, stood up on his hind legs, and looked up the canyon. I also looked but, seeing nothing, pulled the bear down beside me again. For a while he was quiet, but soon stood up again and gazed uneasily up the creek. As nothing appeared I again made him lie down; but there was plainly something on his mind, and at last, after nearly half an hour of these tactics, he jumped to his feet, pushed out his upper lip, and began the blowing sound that he always made when something did not suit him. And there, more than two hundred yards away and wading in the middle of the creek, was a man, fishing. In some way Ben had been aware of his approach long before he had rounded the turn that brought him into sight of our camp.

We remained in Montana long enough to visit the town of Missoula, lay in a supply of provisions, ship our bear-skins, buy a small dog-chain and collar for Ben, who was getting too large for his buck-skin thong, and rest the horses. Then, O'Brien having determined to try his fortune in the mining camps, Spencer and I turned our faces to the West and started back over the same three hundred miles of trackless mountains.

It was well into September when, after many happenings but no serious misadventures, we arrived at a small town on a branch of the Northern Pacific Railway one hundred and twenty-five miles from Spokane; and here we decided to ship not only our new store of furs, but our camp outfit as well. From here on our way lay through open farm lands, and we could find bed and board with the ranchers as we travelled.

Ben was still the same jolly fellow, but now grown so large that by standing on his hind feet he could catch his claws in the hair cinch of the saddle and relieve us of the trouble of lifting him to the back of his mount. He and Jim remained the best of friends. Spencer continued to teach the cub new tricks. Ben could now juggle not only the ball, but any other object that was not too heavy for his strength, and he spent many hours at the pastime. While we were packing the baggage Ben attracted the attention of the entire population. The children, being told that he was gentle, brought him ripe plums and candies and he was constantly stuffed as full as he could hold, and not unnaturally took a great fancy to the kids. They were always ready to play with him, moreover, and his entire time at this place was divided between eating and wrestling with the youngsters. And when we left Ben received an ovation from the whole community.

Ben and Buckskin caused no end of sensations in passing through the country. We often came across loose horses feeding along the highway, and these

Ben tries on his new chain and collar

nearly always wished to make our acquaintance. They would follow Spencer and myself for a while, and then turn back to see if the pony loitering in the rear was not more friendly. And Buck on these occasions would hurry ahead, more than anxious to meet them. But they never waited for an introduction. With loud snorts and tails in the air they either shot away across the open fields or tore madly past us up the turnpike, while Buckskin stood looking after them in puzzled disappointment.

One day, just as we were rounding a turn in the road, we met a farmer and his wife driving a two-horse buggy. Buckskin had just come loping up and was only a few yards behind us, and the sight of a bear riding a horse so pleased the farmer that he paid little attention to his horses, who almost went crazy with fright. Buck looked at the dancing team in amazement, and Ben was as much interested as any one. But the woman, in the very beginning, took sides with the farm team, and sat with terrified eyes clutching her husband's arm and yelling for him to be careful. Finally her fright and cries got on his nerves, and he stopped laughing long enough to shout "WILL YOU SHUT UP?" in a voice that effectually broke up the meeting.

One night we asked for lodging at a farm run by an old lady. As I knocked at the door of the house and proffered our request she at once gave her consent, and directed us to the rear of the stable, where we would find hay for our horses and where we could spread our blankets for the night. Next morning we paid our bill, and as we left the yard the old lady, who was at the door to see us off, called out to know if all five of those horses were ours. I told her that they were and asked what she meant, and she said that she had only charged us for feed for three. She had, she explained, been so taken up with looking at that fool bear riding a horse that two of the horses had escaped her notice.

At last we reached Spokane and Ben's horseback riding came to an end. He had covered more than a thousand miles of mountain and valley and ridden for nearly four months. I fitted up a woodshed for him with a door opening into a small court, where an old partly rotted log was put to remind him of the forest. He soon became a great favorite, and as no one was allowed to tease him he continued to be friendly and gentle.

This shed in which Ben lived had the earth for a floor, and adjoining it there was a carriage-house with a floor some ten or twelve inches above the ground. One day soon after Ben was placed in the shed I came home and found a large pile of fresh earth and a hole leading down under the carriage-house. I could hear Ben digging and puffing at the bottom of it, and when I called he came out, his silky black coat covered with dirt. I had never seen him dig before, unless it was for a root, or the time I had buried him alive to hush his crying in

the little cave in the Bitter Roots; and it was several
days before I understood what he was about. Then
it came to me that he was building himself a winter
home. I have learned since that bears in captivity
by no means always show a desire to hibernate; but
Ben had the instinct thoroughly developed. And
instinct it was, pure and simple, for he had never seen
a bear's den except the one that he left as a tiny cub on
the day that his mother was killed. He evidently
regarded the work as a most serious and important
undertaking, and I watched his labors with much interest. He devoted several hours each day to shaping
his cave and at times would break suddenly away in
the very middle of a romp and hurry to his digging. If
I caught him by his short tail and dragged him out of
the hole, he would rush back to his work as soon as re-
leased. I even enlarged the entrance so that I could
crawl in and watch him work, and on one or two occasions I undertook to help him. But, while he would
not resent this, my work did not seem to please him, as
he moved the dirt which I had dug and resettled it to
suit himself. He piled loose earth up under the floor
of the carriage-house and pushed and jammed it tight
up against the boards until there was not a crack or
space left through which a draught could reach him.
The hole itself he made about four feet in diameter
and about three feet deep; and when this part of the
work was finished he turned his attention to furnishing

his home.   He found some cast-off clothing in the alley near his shed and dragged it into his den under the carriage-house.   After arranging this first instalment he hurried out to look for more, and for several evenings the furnishing of the sleeping apartment occupied the major part of his time.   Once he came back dragging a fine cashmere shawl that he pulled off a clothes-line where one of the neighbors had hung it to air! Not until the floor of his den was several inches deep in rags did he give up foraging and once more return to his usual habits.

And then, one morning, when I went to the shed for kindling, there was no Ben to greet me.   The ground was buried several inches deep in snow and quite a drift had sifted through the crack under the door; and I saw by following Ben's chain that it led down under the carriage-house, and knew that he was now enjoying the comforts that he had made ready a month before.   As long as the severe weather lasted Ben remained in his cave.   But there was nothing either mysterious or curious about his condition.   Sometimes, in the coldest weather, I would call him out and he never failed to come.   It usually took three calls to bring him however.   At my first cry of "Ben!" there would be no sound; then, at a louder "Ben!" there would be a shaking of the chain, then quiet again; but at the third peremptory call there would be a few puffs and snorts and out he would come, fairly steaming from the warmth of his house. I often tried to get him to eat at such times, but he would only smell of the food; then he would stand up on his hind feet with his forepaws against my shoulders, lap my face and hands with his tongue, and crawl back to his nest. Several times I crept down into his den to find out how he slept. He was curled up much as a dog would be and seemed simply to be having a good nap. The amount of heat that his body gave out was astonishing. I have thrust my hand under him as he slept and it actually felt hot. The steam, too, that came up through the cracks of the floor of the carriage-house not only covered the carriage with frost but coated the whole inside of the room.

For more than a year, or until he got so large and rough that he broke the rockers from several chairs that he upset in his mad gallops around the rooms, he was allowed the privilege of the house. He used to stand up and touch the keys of the piano gently, then draw back and listen as long as the vibration lasted. He was fond, too, of being dragged about on his back by a rope that he held fast in his teeth. He never tired of this sport and would get his rope and pester you until you gave him a drag to get rid of him. He had several playthings with which he would amuse himself for hours, and one of these was a block of wood that had replaced the rope ball that he had been used to juggle on his trip through the Bitter Roots. Another was

ten or twelve feet of old garden hose. This he would
seize in his teeth by the middle and shake it as a dog
would shake a snake until the ends fairly snapped.
Once, when he had hold of the hose, I put my mouth
to one end and called through it. He was all attention
at once and when I called again he took the opposite
end in his paws, seated himself squarely on the ground,
and held one eye to the opening to see where the sound
came from. This sitting down to things was characteristic of him. He would never do anything that he
could sit down to until he had deliberately settled himself in that comfortable position. A mirror was a great
puzzle to him and he never fully solved the riddle of
where the other bear kept himself. He would stand
in front and look at his reflection, then try to touch it
with his paw. Finding the glass in the road, he would
tip the mirror forward and look behind it; then start
in and walk several times around it, trying to catch up
with the illusive bear.

But Ben's desire to catch the looking-glass bear was
as nothing to his determination to catch the kitchen
cat. This was his supreme ambition, and, although
he never realized it, there was one occasion on which
he came within sight of success. When he was a
small cub and admitted familiarly to the house he had
often chased the cat around the kitchen until everything
had been upset except the stove; or until the cat,
watching her chance, had escaped to the woodshed to

go into hiding for an hour to get her nerves quieted down. But his final banishment from the house had established a forced truce between them. He was not allowed in her territory, and she took care not to trespass on his. One day, however, when Ben was nearly two years old, he was, for some reason or other, allowed to come into the kitchen for a few moments. And as he entered the room he spied the cat. Instantly his forgotten dreams returned; and when pussy, her tail fluffed up to four times its rightful size, took refuge in the kitchen pantry, Ben very deliberately crossed the kitchen and blocked the pantry door. For a few seconds the two glared at each other and then, with a spit and a yowl, the cat made a mad dash around the pantry shelves and, amid the din of falling stew pans, vaulted clear over the bear's head and crouched by the wood box behind the stove. Now Ben, when a small cub, had been used to going under that stove, and he saw no reason for not taking the same old route. His head went under all right, but for an instant the massive shoulders stuck. Then the powerful hind feet were gathered under him, there was a ripping of linoleum as the sharp nails tore through it, the hind legs straightened out, and the stove went over with a mighty crash. A dozen feet of stove pipe came tumbling down, the room was filled with smoke, and from underneath the wreck a frightened cat leaped through the door closely followed by a disappointed bear. This was Ben's last visit inside the house.

As he grew older and larger, he remained as kindly and good-natured as ever. He would still tumble about with Jim, although the dog could now stand very little of this kind of play; for Ben did not know how strong and rough he was. When, in playing with the boys in back lots, he got warmed up, he would go flying over to a barrel kept full of water for the horses and, climbing upon the rim, would let his hinder parts down into the cool water, turn round up to his chin for a few minutes, and then climb out and take after one of the spectators. When he caught up with any one he would never touch them, but would at once turn and expect them to chase him. Then, when about to be caught, he would go snorting up a telegraph pole. I frequently took him walking in the town, but always on a chain to keep him from chasing everybody. On these occasions if he heard any unfamiliar noise he would clutch the chain close up to his collar and sit down. After listening awhile, if he decided that it was safe to proceed, he would drop the chain and our walk would continue. But if the sound didn't please him he would start for his woodshed on the jump, and after he got to weigh a hundred pounds or more I invariably went with him—if I hung onto the chain.

He still juggled his block, but now he had a new one

A stop for a drink of water

that was more suited to his size and strength, a piece of log a foot or more in diameter and sixteen to eighteen inches in length. This stick he kept for a couple of years and juggled so much that his claws wore hollows in the ends of it.

When Ben was four years old business compelled me to move to the town of Missoula, Montana. I could not bear to part with my pet, so shipped him by express to the town he had visited on horseback as a tiny cub. Now, however, the express company charged me for transportation on three hundred and thirty-two pounds of bear meat. It was fall when we moved to Missoula, and Ben was given a small room in one end of a woodshed and, as he had no cave to sleep in, I had the room filled with shavings. Ben's arrival was quite an event and roused much interest among the younger element of the town; which at first was shown by about forty boys attacking him with sticks and anything that they could hurl at him or punch him with. I showed them, however, how gentle and playful he was; got some of the boys to wrestle with him; told them that if they continued this rough treatment to which Ben was not used I would be compelled to lock him up; and, having had some experience with boys as well as with bears, forbore to tell them what I proposed to do to those who did not listen to me. This explanation and Ben's evident readiness to make friends quite changed the general attitude toward him, but there were a few who refused to see things from my point of view. There was a man in Missoula at that time, Urlin by name, who was, or thought he was, the whole show. He was a sort of incipient "boss"; was at the head of the city council, and took it upon himself to see that things in general were run according to his ideas. He had two red-headed sons who aspired to occupy a similar position among the boys, and these had been the ringleaders of the mob that had attacked Ben, and were among the few who either could not or would not abandon the tactics of teasing and persecution. So, as there was no lock on Ben's shed, but only a wooden button, and as it was already late in the fall, I nailed this fast and left the bear in his bed of shavings. That same afternoon, happening to look out of the window of the shop in which I was working, I saw people hurrying down the street and went to the door to find out what the excitement was about. Two blocks away, in front of my house, a mob was gathering, and I hurried home to find most of the women of the neighborhood wringing their hands and calling down all kinds of curses on my head.

At first I could make neither head nor tail of the clamor, but finally gathered that that bloodthirsty, savage, and unspeakable bear of mine had killed a boy; and upon asking to see the victim was told that the remains had been taken to a neighbor's house and a doctor summoned. This was scarcely pleasant news and not calculated to make me popular in my new home; but, knowing that whatever had happened Ben had not taken the offensive without ample cause, I unchained him and put him into the cellar of my house, well out of harm's way, before looking further into the matter. Then I went over to the temporary morgue and found the corpse (needless to say it was one of the Urlin boys) sitting up on the kitchen floor holding a sort of an impromptu reception and, with the exception of Ben, the least excited of any one concerned. I could not help admiring the youngster's pluck, for he was an awful sight. From his feet to his knees his legs were lacerated and his clothing torn into shreds; and the top of his head—redder by far than ever nature had intended—was a bloody horror. As soon as I laid eyes on him I guessed what had happened.

It developed that the two Urlin boys had broken open the door of the shed and gone in to wrestle with the bear. Ben was willing, as he always was, and a lively match was soon on; whereupon, seeing that the bear did not harm the two already in the room, another of the boys joined the scuffle. Then one of them got on the bear's back. This was a new one on Ben, but he took kindly to the idea and was soon galloping around the little room with his rider. Then another boy climbed on and Ben carried the two of them at the same mad pace. Then the third boy got aboard and round they all went, much to the delight of themselves and their cheering audience in the doorway. But even Ben's muscles of steel had their limit of endurance, and after a few circles of the room with the three riders he suddenly stopped and rolled over on his back. And now an amazing thing happened. Of the three boys, suddenly tumbled helter-skelter from their seats, one happened to fall upon the upturned paws of the bear; and Ben, who for years had juggled rope balls, cord sticks, and miniature logs, instantly undertook to give an exhibition with his new implement. Gathering the badly frightened boy into position, the bear set him whirling. His clothing from his shoe tops to his knees was soon ripped to shreds and his legs torn and bleeding; his scalp was lacerated by the sharp claws until the blood flew in showers; his cries rose to shrieks and sank again to moans; but the bear, unmoved, kept up the perfect rhythm of his strokes. Finally the terrified lookers-on in the doorway, realizing that something had to be done if their leader was not to be twirled to death before their eyes, tore a rail from the fence and with a few pokes in Ben's side induced him to drop the boy, who was then dragged out apparently more dead than alive.

Dr. Buckley, of the Northern Pacific Railway Hospital, carried young Urlin to his office, shaved his head, took seventy-six stitches in his scalp, and put rolls of surgical plaster on his shins. So square and true had Ben juggled him that not a scratch was found on his face or on any part of his body between the top of his head and his knees. He eventually came out of the hospital no worse for his ordeal, but I doubt if he ever again undertook to ride a bear.

For a while there was much curiosity in town as to what old man Urlin would do in the matter, and many prophecies and warnings reached me. But for some days I heard nothing from him. Then he called on me and asked, very politely, if I had killed the bear. When I told him that Ben was well and would in all natural probability live for twenty years or so, the old fellow threw diplomacy to the winds and fumed and threatened like a madman. But he calmed down in the end; especially after he was informed by his lawyers that, as his boys had forcibly broken into my shed, it was he himself that could be called to legal account. And so the matter was dropped.

But Ben was now grown so large that none but myself cared to wait on him; and when, the next spring, I found that I was going to be away in the mountains all summer, I began looking about for some way of getting him a good home. Nothing in the world would have induced me to have him killed, and I did not like to turn him loose in the hills for some trapper to catch or poison. Moreover I doubted his ability, after so sheltered a life, to shift for himself in the wilderness. But this was a problem in which the "don't's" were more easily discovered than the "do's."

Weeks slipped by, I was leaving in a short time, no solution had offered, and I was at my wits' end. And then a travelling circus came to town. I sought out the manager, told him Ben's story, obtained his promise of kind treatment and good care for my pet and, with genuine heartache, presented the fine animal to him. That was sixteen years ago and I have never heard of Ben since. I often wonder if he's still alive and if he'd know me. But of the last I have not a single doubt.

THE BLACK BEAR

Its Distribution and Habits

CLASSIFICATION OF BEARS

SCIENTIFIC naturalists, like other learned gentlemen in large spectacles, have a way (or it sometimes seems as though they had) of using very big words about very small matters. For instance, what they might describe as "an aquatic larva of *Rana catesbiana* or other Batrachian," we would call a tadpole. And so on through the list. But we are obliged to assume that they have excellent reasons for their choice of language, and there is no getting around the fact that if we wish to profit by their wisdom we have to learn at least the simple rules of their speech.

We ought, for example, to understand that when a new animal, or a new variety of an old one, is discovered, or rather when it is officially described and listed by a naturalist, it is given a special Latin name which, added to the Latin name of the family to which it belongs, thenceforth serves to identify it among all students of natural history. Moreover, as a compliment to the man who thus stood god-parent for it in the scientific world, his name is added, in parentheses, to these Latin designations. Thus the Rocky Mountain grizzly bear is known to technical fame as *Ursus hor-*

ribilis (Ord), which, being interpreted, means that this much-misrepresented member of the bear tribe was first described officially by George Ord and was named by him "The Terrible."

There have been many attempts to classify the North American bears; and from time to time, as new facts come to light, or new students advance new theories as to the relationships of the different species, these lists are altered. But before proceeding to give my own observations upon the actual habits and characteristics of the common Black Bear, the *Ursus americanus* (Pallas) of the text-books, I reproduce (without recourse) a list of what appear to be the most generally recognized varieties of bears inhabiting the North American continent.

The Polar Bear. *Ursus maritimus* (Desm.). Polar regions generally.

THE ALASKAN BROWN BEARS

The Kadiak Bear. *Ursus middendorffi* (Merriam). Kadiak Island, Alaska. The largest of all living bears.

The Yakutat Bear. *Ursus dalli* (Merriam). Yakutat Bay and seaward slopes of the St. Elias range.

The Admiralty Bear. *Ursus eulophus* (Merriam). Admiralty Islands, Alaska.

The Peninsula Bear. *Ursus merriami* (Allen). Portage Bay, Alaska Peninsula.

The Rocky Mountain Grizzly. *Ursus horribilis* (Ord). Rocky Mountains from Mexico to Alaska.

The Sonora Grizzly. *Ursus horribilis horriœus* (Baird). South-western New Mexico.

The Barren Ground Grizzly. *Ursus richardsoni* (Mayne Reid). Great Slave Lake regions and Barren Grounds.

The American Black Bear. *Ursus americanus* (Pallas).

Scornborger's Black Bear. *Ursus americanus scornborgeri* (Bangs). Labrador.

Queen Charlotte Islands Black Bear. *Ursus americanus carlottœ* (Osgood).

Desert Black Bear. *Ursus americanus eremicus* (Merriam). Coahuila, Mexico.

Florida Black Bear. *Ursus floridanus* (Merriam).

Louisiana Black Bear. *Ursus luteolus* (Griffith).

North-western Black Bear. *Ursus altifrontalis* (Elliot). Clallam County, Washington.

Alberta Black Bear. *Ursus hylodromus* (Elliot).

The Fighting Bear. *Ursus machetes* (Elliot). Chihuahua, Mexico.

Emmons's Glacier Bear. *Ursus emmonsi* (Dall). Mt. St. Elias region, Alaska.

The Inland White Bear. *Ursus kermodii* (Hornaday). South-western British Columbia.

DESCRIPTION AND DISTRIBUTION

THE American Black Bear, or, as our friends with the big spectacles have named him, *Ursus americanus* (Pallas), has by very long odds the widest distribution of any North American bear.

The polar bear stays well inside the Arctic Circle. The big brown Alaskan bears are only found in certain localities on or near the north-west coast of the continent. The grizzlies inhabit, or inhabited, the mountain regions of the extreme west from Mexico to Alaska. But the Black Bear is found in the central and northern parts of the United States and in the central and southern parts of Canada from the Atlantic coast to the shore of the Pacific Ocean; and his half brothers, or first cousins, or whatever they are, in Florida, Louisiana, Texas, and Old Mexico, are so much like him that it takes a specialist and sometimes a post-mortem examination to tell them apart.

I have watched and studied these animals in the open for nearly thirty years, and have played eavesdropper and Peeping Tom times out of number when they were unconscious of my presence; and yet I have had dealings with Black Bears in Texas and Old Mexico whom I would never for a moment have suspected of differing in blood or descent from their northern relatives. However, as we may see from the list already given, the Black Bears of Florida, Louisiana, Mexico, and certain restricted districts in the North, have been technically recognized as entitled to separate classification. And it is just as well to state clearly that in these pages all statements (unless otherwise indicated) refer to the common American Black Bear, and the term Black Bear, when unqualified, refers always to *Ursus americanus* (Pallas).

It is also just as well to call attention in the beginning to a mistaken idea that is a very old one and is very generally entertained about these animals. I refer to the belief that there is a difference of species between the black and the brown or cinnamon-colored individuals of the tribe. This notion is so wide-spread that one often hears it stated that there are three varieties of bears in the United States: the Black Bear, the Cinnamon Bear, and the Grizzly. But this is a most misleading statement. There are many cinnamon-colored bears, but there is no such species as the Cinnamon Bear. Some Black Bears are brown, and so are some grizzlies. Some Black Bears are cinnamon-color, and so are some grizzlies. But the difference between the Black Bears that are black and the Black Bears that are cinnamon-color is the difference between blondes and brunettes; while the difference between a brown-colored grizzly and a brown-colored Black Bear is like the difference between a brown cocker spaniel and a brown setter—one of breed.

The Black Bear has a head broader between the ears in proportion to its length and a muzzle much shorter and sharper than the grizzly. This muzzle is also almost invariably of a grayish or buff color. The animal shows a rather noticeable hump over the small of its back, just in front of the hind legs, and these legs are less straight than those of the grizzly and more sloping at the haunches. Its ears are larger. Its eyes are small and pig-like. Its claws are short, much curved, very stocky at the base, and taper rapidly to a sharp point. They are far less formidable as weapons and far less serviceable as digging implements than the long, slightly curved, blunt claws of the grizzly; but they are perfectly adapted to the uses to which their owner puts them. And the chief of these uses is climbing.

The Black Bear climbs, literally, like a squirrel; and from cubhood to old age spends a considerable portion of his time in trees. He can climb as soon as he can walk and his mother takes clever advantage of the fact. She sends her cubs up a tree whenever she wants them off her hands for a time—uses trees, indeed, very much as human mothers who have no one to watch their children while they work use day nurseries. The first thing a Black Bear mother does when any danger threatens is to send her cubs up a tree. She will then frequently try to induce the enemy to follow her and, when she has eluded him, will return for the cubs. In parts of the country where there are grizzlies, or where there are wolves, she will generally thus dispose of her children before herself going off to feed on berries or other provender. In all my experience I have never known cubs, when thus ordered into retirement by their mother, to come down from the selected tree until she called them. They will climb to the extreme top; run out to the ends of all the branches in turn, chase each other up and down the trunk, and finally curl up in some convenient fork and go to sleep. But though it may be hours before the old bear comes back for them nothing will induce them to set foot on the ground until she comes.

Later in life the Black Bear continues to regard trees as its natural refuge from all dangers. They will invariably "tree" when pursued by dogs, chased by a man on horseback, or otherwise threatened. And a few years ago I witnessed an amusing incident which shows that these are not the only circumstances under which a Black Bear thinks to find safety in its favorite refuge. I was engaged at the time in trying to get some flash-light photographs of grizzlies, and one afternoon, soon after I had gotten my apparatus set up and was waiting for darkness and the appearance of my expected sitters, a violent thunderstorm came up. I had just covered my camera and flash-pan with bark peeled from a couple of small saplings and taken shelter myself under a thick, umbrella-like tree, when I saw a small Black Bear coming through the woods and headed straight for my hiding place. At every flash of lightning he paused and made a dash for the nearest tree, but by the time he got there the flash would be over and he would start on again. Finally, there came a blinding streak of jagged fire, accompanied by a splitting crash, and the small bear made one jump into the tree that happened to be nearest him, went hand over hand to the extreme top, rolled himself into a little ball with his nose between his paws, and never moved until the storm had gone by.

But the Black Bear also resorts to trees of his own accord, using them as a loafing place and even as a sleeping apartment. I have seen one lying prone on his back on a big limb, all four feet in the air, as utterly comfortable and care-free as a fat man in a hammock.

In regions where the grizzly and the Black Bear are both found, the Black Bear spends much of his leisure among the branches and often has special trees that he uses as sleeping quarters. Some of these, from constant use, become as deeply scarred and worn as an old wooden sidewalk in a lumbering town; and I have seen them that appeared to have been used for years.

One sometimes hears it claimed that a Black Bear can only climb a tree around which he can conveniently clasp his front legs, man-fashion. They can climb, and that with almost equal ease, any tree that will hold their weight; from a sapling so small that there is just room for them to sink one set of hind claws above the other in a straight line, to an old giant so big that they can only cling to its face, squirrel-fashion, and behind the trunk of which (also squirrel-fashion) they can hide, circling as you walk around it.

Another curious fact about the Black Bear's sharp claws is that these invariably match their owner's hide in color. A black animal always has black claws. A brown one has brown claws. A cinnamon-colored one has cinnamon-colored claws. This is not true of the grizzly. And since, as we will see later, the color of an individual bear often changes with the weathering of its coat, one can approximate the normal, or new-coat, color of the animal from the color of its claws.

In order to show more clearly than mere words could do the character of the Black Bear's claws and their differences from those of the grizzly, I have photographed a front and hind foot of each animal and also the corresponding tracks made on the ground, and these photographs are here reproduced for comparison and reference. The difference in the fore paws will be seen at a glance; the long, blunt, four-and-a-half to six-inch claws of the grizzly serving to distinguish them unmistakably from the short, sharp, one to one-and-a-half-inch claws of the Black Bear. The hind paws are more nearly alike; but one notices at once how markedly both differ from the front paws and how nearly they approximate to *feet*. This is true of all bears.

As, in the West, these two bears are often found in the same localities, and as one of the first things an observer of them should learn is to distinguish between their tracks, I shall point out some of the more salient differences between the two.

On the fore paw of the Black Bear the pad is noticeably rounded in front and somewhat hollowed out behind and is, in a general way, rather kidney-shaped. It does not show the dent that is so plainly seen on the outside of the grizzly's front paw, and the front edge of it is much narrower. Also, when the track is perfect, the distance between the impress of the toes and the impress of the tips of the claws is much less.

On the hind paw of the Black Bear the front of the pad is also more rounded than that of the grizzly and the heel is blunt instead of pointed. Another difference in shape is shown by the fact that a straight line drawn through the middle toe and along the axis of the foot will, in the Black Bear's track, exactly hit the heel, while in the grizzly's track it will fall well to the outside of the heel. The Black Bear's hind paw is also more deeply dented at the instep than that of the grizzly.

The feet of the Black Bear are stockier than those of the grizzly and more powerfully muscled—probably as

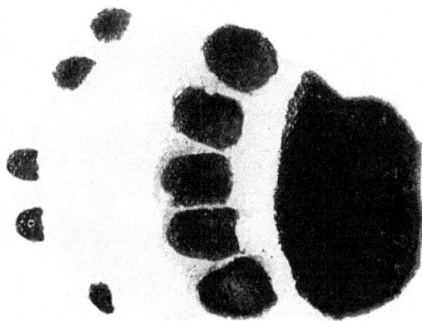

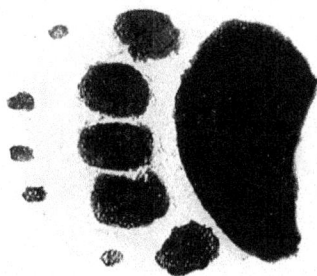

1. Front foot of a black bear
2. Front track of a black bear
   Size, 5 × 4 inches

3. Front foot of a grizzly bear
4. Front track of a grizzly bear
   Size, 8 × 4½ inches

a result of the animal's climbing habits. On the other hand their fore legs do not show the wonderful muscular development that is one of the marked characteristics of *Ursus horribilis*.

The Black Bear received its name informally, as it were, from the early settlers of New England, where the overwhelming majority of the species happened to be black and where, by dint of saying, "I saw a black bear in the woods this afternoon," people came to refer to the animal as the Black Bear. Later on the name was sanctioned by scientific baptism and the animal became officially known as the American Black Bear. The designation, however, as we have seen, is by no means universally descriptive. In the East, and in the Middle West, an occasional brown specimen is met with. But when the Rocky Mountain region is reached there is a bewildering variation in the coloring of the species. The majority of the breed are still black, but at least a quarter and perhaps a third of the specimens met with show a different coloration. Of these probably the seal-browns are the most numerous; but I have seen Black Bears of every conceivable shade, from a light cream color, through the yellow browns, to a jet and glossy black never seen in the East. One animal that I watched for some weeks in the mountains of Wyoming was of a curious olive yellow from tip to tail. In north-western Montana and north-eastern Idaho one used to see many mouse-colored, or steel-blue-colored,

Black Bears; and around Flat Head Lake, in Montana, I have seen a number of albinos. Curiously enough, albino deer used to be found in this same locality. One sometimes hears it declared that the "true" Black Bear has a white horseshoe on its breast. This is simply a distortion of the fact that many Black Bears, especially black ones, have a "white vest," varying from a few white hairs to a spot six inches square. Now and then one sees a star, or a shield, or some other oddly shaped mark, and sometimes instead of being white these are cream color or a dirty yellow.

Like the grizzly, the individual Black Bear may vary in color according to the season, the age of its coat, and the weathering that this has undergone. An animal that is a glossy black in the fall may, by the early summer of the following year, be a rusty black; or one that is a rich brown when it first emerges from its winter sleep, may be a faded yellow brown when it has shed its fur and only its hair remains in the beginning of the next summer. But, as far as my observation goes, these changes of color are wholly the result of sun bleach, weathering, and wear and tear.

All fur-bearing animals have both fur and hair—the long guard-hair completely covering and protecting the fine fur underneath. This is of course true of the Black Bear, and it is interesting to note how both hair and fur are changed each year, yet without ever

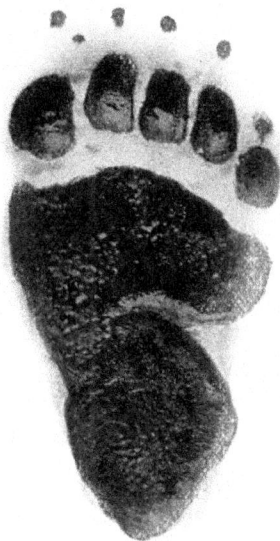

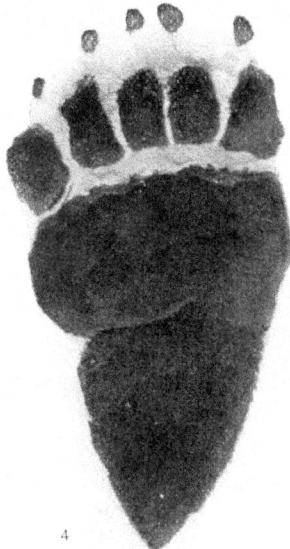

1. Hind foot of a black bear
2. Hind track of a black bear
    Size, 8 × 4 inches

3. Hind foot of a grizzly bear
4. Hind track of a grizzly bear
    Size, 10 × 5½ inches

leaving the animal uncovered. About a month after the bear comes out of its winter den the fur begins to drop out, first on the legs and belly, and then on the other parts of the body. During this time the animal takes great satisfaction in scratching itself on stumps and bushes—straddling them on its walks and returning again and again to repeat the operation. From then on the old coat gradually falls out—fur and hair, and at one stage the falling coat hangs in shreds and gives the bear a most wretched and moth-eaten appearance. Meanwhile the new hair is coming in, but not as yet the new fur, so that by early summer the bear has a new suit of clothes, but no underwear. As fall approaches the new fur begins to grow. And by the time the animal is ready to den up for the winter he has a full new coat. This continues to grow during hibernation and a bear's coat is at its best when the animal first reappears in the spring.

The full-grown Black Bear is, of course, very much smaller than the full-grown grizzly, but it is rather difficult to give any close figures for what might be called a normal specimen. The largest Black Bear that I ever actually weighed, myself, tipped the scales at four hundred and sixty-two pounds. There had been much discussion about this bear, and guesses, before weighing, ranged from three hundred to seven hundred pounds. This gives a good idea of the danger of putting much faith in the estimates of people who have merely seen an animal in the open, and have no actual data for comparison and upon which to base their opinion. I have, first and last, weighed a good many Black Bears, and should say that, when full grown, they range in weight from say two hundred and fifty to say five hundred pounds. In some instances they probably go over that. As a rule the largest specimens I have seen appeared to be in the prime of life and in the best of condition, but I have seen those that gave every evidence of being old and almost decrepit that would not have weighed over two hundred and fifty pounds.

Ben, when I caught him, was about three months old, and would have weighed about five or six pounds. When he was a year old he weighed about fifty pounds. The last time I actually put him on the scales he weighed three hundred and thirty-two pounds, and I believe that four months later, when I gave him away, he would have gone better than four hundred. This three hundred and thirty-two pounds was actual live weight.

What may be the life span of the Black Bear in their free state it is hard to say. They do not arrive at full maturity or growth until their sixth or seventh year, and they probably live well beyond the twenty-five year mark. Mr. William R. Lodge and his father of Cuyahoga Falls, Ohio, have a pair of Black Bears that they have had for twenty-two years, that were six months old when they got them, and that are still healthy and vigorous. There is no reason to suppose that a free animal would not live at least as long as one confined under unnatural conditions.

In the case of the grizzly I have known and watched for years an individual bear in his home mountains that must have been more than twenty years old and that was still in full vigor the last time I saw him. But I have never happened to keep similar track of any individual Black Bear in the open. I have, however, never seen any Black Bear that looked as old as some grizzlies I have seen.

It is a curious fact that in twenty-seven years of coming and going in the joint territory of the grizzly and the Black Bear I have never once come upon the bones or the carcass of a grizzly that had died a natural death. I have, on the other hand, in dens and elsewhere, seen many Black Bear carcasses and skeletons. Once, in the Selkirks, in British Columbia, for instance, we back-tracked a Black Bear to the winter den that it had just left, and in this den we found the skeleton of another Black Bear. The one that had wintered there had raked the bones away and had made its bed alongside of them.

CHARACTERISTICS AND HABITS

In this chapter I purpose to bring together in some sort of order the characteristic habits of the Black Bear as I have personally observed them during many years of life in the open. Of course it is never possible to watch a single wild animal from the time it is born until it grows up, lives its natural life out, and dies; nor even to follow one through the activities of an ordinary year of its life. And even if one could do this, one would have to be very careful not to generalize too broadly from the actions of a single individual. But by the time one has seen thousands of Black Bear, let us say, in many parts of their range, in all stages of growth, at all seasons of the year, in undisturbed enjoyment of their liberty, and free to follow their own instincts of work and play, one is able, by putting two and two together, to piece out a pretty accurate knowledge of the species.

One gets, also, a good working understanding of what traits are characteristic of all the normal specimens of the race, of what habits are dependent upon local conditions and vary as these alter, and of what actions are attributable to the personal dispositions of individual

68

animals. For all animals are like men in this, that in minor matters their habits vary with the conditions under which they live, and that in still less noticeable ways the bearing of different individuals under similar circumstances is determined by their personal characters.

What follows in the present chapter, then, is a summing up of the general habits and race characteristics of the Black Bear; and all statements that are not qualified are, in my experience, observable of these animals wherever found.

Of course we all know that the Black Bear is an hibernating animal. That is to say that in most, if not in all, parts of its widely distributed range, it passes a portion of the year asleep and without food or drink, in a den or some sort of make-shift shelter. We shall have much to say later on about this strange habit, and about some of the queer notions people have about it, but we only mention it here because, since little bears are born during the time their mother is in winter quarters, it is necessary to establish winter quarters for them to be born in.

Black Bear cubs, then, are born in the winter den of the mother some time from the latter half of January to the middle of March, according to the latitude and also according to the altitude of the den. The further north a bear happens to live, and the higher up in the hills it happens to live, the later the spring sets in and so the later the animal comes out of its retirement. And the cubs are born from six weeks to two months before the mother comes out.

The little Black Bears, when first born, are absurdly small and pitifully helpless. Their eyes, like those of puppies and kittens, are shut and do not open for some time. They have no teeth and are almost naked, and although the mother may weigh as much as four hundred pounds or more, the whole litter of cubs does not weigh over a couple of pounds, and single cubs vary from eight to eighteen ounces in weight, according to the number in the litter. A Black Bear will have all the way from one to four cubs at a time, and four is not at all uncommon. I have never seen but two grizzlies with four cubs, but I have seen a great many Black Bears with that many. Three, however, seems to be the common number throughout the Rocky Mountain region. Of course meeting a Black Bear in the woods with only one cub, even in the early spring, does not definitely prove that she only gave birth to one; because the others might have died or have been killed. But the records of Black Bears in captivity show that single cubs are not unknown.

The young cubs at first are delicate and for a week or two the mother never leaves them, but curls around them and keeps them warm and broods them. They seem, however, to have excellent lungs, for one can hear them whimper if one has located a bear's hiding place and approaches it after the cubs are born, an experience that I have had more than once in the mountains. The Messrs. Lodge, of Cuyahoga Falls, Ohio, have supplied their bears with artificial hibernating dens dug in the side of a hill where their bear pit is situated. These are supplied with ventilating shafts, and the owners, for a number of years, have been able to determine the exact date of the birth of a litter, by listening for the querulous voices of the cubs. These gentlemen, by the way, have endeavored in all possible regards to approximate natural conditions in furnishing accommodations for their captive animals; with the result that they have been among the few successful raisers of Black Bears. I will have occasion to refer more than once to the records which these gentlemen have kept during their twenty years' experience.

For some time, then, after the cubs are born, the family continues shut up in the winter den; but, unlike the grizzly, they frequently, toward the end, leave their shelter before they are ready to abandon it for good. I have seen cases where a Black Bear mother and cubs came out in deep snow, and after wandering about for several miles went back again for a full two weeks before coming out for good. In some cases the mother will come out on these preliminary excursions before the young are able to walk. But they do not either habitually or finally abandon the den until they can get down to the bottoms where the snow is gone and the vegetation has started sprouting. This, by the way, if you happen to live in the neighborhood, is an excellent time to keep a sharp watch on your young pigs.

At this stage the cubs weigh about five or six pounds and, although it is some months before they begin to forage at all for themselves, their development is now much more rapid. I have frequently watched old Black Bears with cubs in the early summer, but have never seen the young ones show any apparent interest in what the mother was eating, and hence I believe that in their natural state they are six or seven months old before they begin the process of being weaned. But although about the time the berries are ripe the cubs take to foraging pretty generally on their own account, they continue to nurse right through the summer and until they either den up with the mother in the fall or, as I think is more usual, until they are turned adrift by her before she herself dens up alone. In fact I have seen them, late in the year, and when they were of a size that should have made them ashamed of such dependence, pestering their mother as she walked, and getting occasional cuffs for their persistence.

Ben showed no concern whatever over grown-up bear dishes until the berry season came around, when he suddenly developed an appetite for outside board, and not only seemed to want all the various things the hills provided, but would howl lustily if he did not get them.

The Black Bear, while not much of a traveller, wanders over a fairly wide range in search of various foods in their season; yet, broadly speaking, is pretty apt to live and die in the general neighborhood of its birth. They wander both day and night, although when they are in a region where grizzlies are also to be found they are careful to disappear about the time that the latter, which are much more nocturnal in habit, may be expected to come out. When a Black Bear has young cubs she will stay for a week or two at a time in one place, and will scratch a nest or bed among the leaves or in a thicket and lie up there between feeds with her youngsters.

There are few things more interesting than to watch a bear with her cubs when she thinks herself alone. They are the gayest and most playful little balls of fur, and she will let them maul her and worry her and pretend to fight her. But a Black Bear does not, as the grizzly does, talk to her cubs all the time. A grizzly will walk along through the woods with two or three cubs carrying on what appears to be a connected conversation. She grunts and whines and makes noises at them that sound as though they were full of advice and admonition. They are doubtless merely encouragement or assurances of her presence. But the Black Bear is silent except in cases of danger or emergency. Then she, too, "speaks" to her youngsters, and they never seem to be at a loss for her meaning. At any rate they go up a tree at the word of command, and come down again at the grunt that means, "All right now, come on."

As the cubs grow larger and stronger the mother wanders farther afield with them, and, from sacrificing all her time and desires to their needs and safety, comes gradually first to tolerate, and toward the end of the season rather to resent, their persistent demands upon her.   One imagines that it is with a final indifference and relief that she sends them off to shift for themselves.   For, like other animals, a bear, while showing the most devoted and courageous love for her children while they are helpless, has a very short-lived affection for them once they cease to need her protection.   In one instance the Lodges tried the experiment of returning some half-grown cubs to their mother after a comparatively short separation, during which she and her mate had been together in the main pit.   The two cubs had only been by themselves for a few weeks, and before they were finally returned to the pen with their mother they were kept for some days separated from her by nothing more than an iron grating.   Yet as soon as they were put into the pit with her she seized one of them and killed it, and was starting up her exercise tree after the other which had

A mother and two cubs

taken refuge there when the owners interfered and rescued the youngster. Here, as I see it, was a case of artificial separation which, once the mother had accepted, placed her, as far as her own feelings went, in exactly the same frame of mind toward her cubs as though she had abandoned them in the natural course of things and their company had afterward been forced upon her.

Neither the Black Bear nor the grizzly is really a sociable animal, but free Black Bears occasionally play together, which grizzlies never seem to do. Under ordinary circumstances, however, Black Bears have a funny trick of pretending not to see each other when they meet. If one of them comes into a marshy meadow or a small open glade in the woods where one or two others are already feeding, he will make the most laughable pretence of not seeing them. He will stop at the edge of the opening and go through all the motions of examining the country, carefully looking, however, everywhere but in the direction of the other bears; all of which is vastly amusing to one familiar with the keenness of his senses and the alertness of his attention, and the practical impossibility of getting within seeing or hearing distance of him without his knowing it. Meanwhile the bears already on the ground play their part in the little comedy with all the good will in the world. They have undoubtedly been aware of the approach of the newcomer long before any human watcher of the scene could have suspected it. But they give no outward sign of being aware of the new arrival. If, however, the intruder had happened to have been a grizzly they would undoubtedly have taken to their heels or taken refuge in the nearest tree with loud puffings and snortings some minutes before he reached the scene. Yet these same bears, once they have fed their fill, will frequently go to playing together as one never sees the grizzlies do. Two of them will stand up and wrestle, roll each other over and over, chase each other about, and generally have a fine romp. As a rule, however, this sort of play takes place between bears of different sizes, and the smaller one sometimes gets well thrown about and mauled.

One of the most entertaining experiences that I ever had in the woods was connected with just such an after-dinner romp between two Black Bears. I was photographing grizzlies in the Rocky Mountains in Wyoming, and had set up my camera and flash-light apparatus near a likely looking trail. My flash-pan was placed on top of a ten-foot pole stuck in the ground under a small pine tree, and a fine wire was run from the switch that operated the apparatus across the trail and tied to a convenient bush. I had completed my arrangements about half-past four in the afternoon and had concealed myself in a mass of fallen timber some seventy-five or eighty feet away prepared to wait for dusk.

Soon after I got settled I noticed two Black Bears in a little clearing to my left and, for something to do, I set to watching them. For some time they fed quietly here and there and then they took to playing. One of them was quite a bit larger than the other, but the smaller one was game and though he got considerably the worst of the rough sport they kept the play up for quite a while. Suddenly, however, in the very midst of an excited wrestling match, the little fellow drew away, stood up on his hind legs and listened for a moment, and then went up a convenient tree, his companion following his example and taking refuge in another one. I was much interested over this turn of affairs and kept a close watch to see what was going to happen next. But, after quite a little wait, the bears seemed to make up their minds that it had been a false alarm and, coming down from their respective trees, they resumed their rough and tumble fun. Not for long, however. It was only a minute or two before they repeated their former maneuvres, and this time they appeared to have no doubt as to the imminence of danger. They had worked their way over to my side of the clearing, and when they broke for shelter the little bear took refuge in the small pine tree under which my flash-pan stood, his companion selecting a larger tree a little further away. And sure enough, almost as soon as they were well off the ground an old grizzly came stalking dignifiedly out of the woods and down the trail upon which my camera was set. But he had evidently noticed that something questionable was going on, and he walked over toward the tree where the larger bear was sitting. The latter, conscious of his advantage of position, greeted the grizzly's approach with a volley of puffs and snorts, and after looking around him in a disdainful sort of way, the grizzly sauntered over toward the smaller bear's tree, where the same performance was gone through. Here, however, the grizzly found something that aroused his curiosity more keenly than a mere Black Bear, for he discovered my pole and flash-pan. He stood up on his hind legs and easily sniffed the top of the pan and then, discovering the wire, he followed it without touching it away from the pine tree and across the trail to where it was fastened. Then, his curiosity getting the better of him, he raised one front paw and pulled the bush toward him, whereupon the charge of powder exploded with a huge puff of smoke, and as I stood up in my retreat to get a better view of the outcome I caught a glimpse with one eye of a big grizzly turning a double back somersault, while with the other I saw a small Black Bear take one desperate leap from the branches of his pine tree and disappear into the wood in huge leaps.

When the last act of this little comedy began I had risen to my feet in order to get a clear view of what took place, and when the smaller Black Bear had disappeared into the woods I saw that his larger companion had become aware of my presence. I once more concealed myself among the branches, but the Black Bear in the tree kept an eye in my direction and when, at the end of five minutes or so, the smaller bear returned cautiously to the scene of his recent discomfiture and began to coax his friend to come down and resume their play, it was amusing to watch the cross-purposes at which they found themselves. For the one up the tree who knew of my presence was afraid to come down and yet unable to explain the circumstances to the one on the ground, and he in his turn was utterly unable to make head or tail of the other's actions. He finally gave up the attempt to persuade him and wandered away into the woods, and at the end of half an hour or so the other bear, evidently with serious misgivings, came carefully down the opposite side of his tree and made off at the double quick.

The Black Bear's habits of hibernation are less rigid and apparently less developed than the grizzly's. To begin with, they are far less industrious in providing themselves with a den, and less particular in having it weatherproof and well concealed. The grizzly habitually seeks out some natural cave or shelter in the rocks, high up in the mountains, often above snow line. This he prepares for occupancy by raking into it whatever he can find in the way of leaves or dried grasses, and sometimes stops up with earth and stones such holes or openings as would expose the interior to the weather. The Black Bear is far less particular. Any old place that offers him some fair promise of protection and privacy seems good enough for him. He dens up at much lower altitudes, goes into winter quarters later and comes out much earlier. One of his favorite devices is to dig a hole under the butt end of a fallen tree, rake a few leaves into the opening, and then crawl in himself. Sometimes, when the tree is a good-sized one and the roots hold the butt of it a little clear of the ground, he is saved the trouble of digging at all and makes a sort of nest in the space beneath the trunk. At other times he will dig a hole in the soft ground, and, of course, occasionally uses caves or other natural retreats if he happens to find them handy. Ben, it will be recalled, dug under the floor of my barn when it came to be his bedtime.

The time for denning up varies with the locality and the weather, and throughout the North-west is anywhere from November 1 to January 1. Unlike the grizzly, however, the Black Bear will often come out for a while if a warm spell follows his denning up. The Lodges note that their bears, once they are settled in their winter caves, never seem to pay any further attention to the weather. But while this is probably the rule, I have seen Black Bears out in some numbers late in December after there had been severe freezing weather during which all bears had denned up.

There is some difference of opinion as to their habits further south, and some authorities claim that at the extreme southern limit of their range the bears belonging to the Black Bear group do not hibernate at all. I incline, however, from what I have seen—or rather failed to see—to the opposite belief; for in parts of Old Mexico where, in the spring, I have seen many bears, I have again in the winter time failed to see either them or their fresh tracks, and upon making inquiry of the Indians have been told that they were asleep.

Moreover, Mr. Charles Sheldon, of New York, who for fifteen years has made a close study of bears in their natural state and has spent four years in Mexico studying bear and sheep, informs me that all the bears den up almost as early in those mountains as they do further north, and that he has never seen bears in Mexico come out of winter quarters earlier than in the United States.

There has been much scientific discussion as to the nature of this long sleep, and also much popular misconception in regard to its outward manifestations. I do not aspire to a voice in the former, but can speak from considerable experience in regard to the latter. Many, perhaps most, people seem to think that a bear that has denned up for the winter is in some mysterious, and more or less complete state of coma; that its breathing is all but suspended, and that it would be difficult, even by violence, to rouse it. They are very far from the truth. Bears sleep, but are easily roused, quick to scent danger, and ready to abandon their retreat and look up a new one if they think it necessary.

Ben, at any time during the winter, would rouse if I called him, and would even come to the mouth of his lair for a moment to greet me. I could, moreover, hear him breathing, and sometimes hear him move and readjust himself to a more comfortable position. He was a very lazy, stupid, sleepy bear; but never too stupid or sleepy to answer my call.

One fall in Washington, near Colville in the Calispell Mountains, while after deer, I noticed a strange mass of dead leaves, small sticks, pine needles, and other forest refuse gathered under the tangled trunks of a windfall, where a number of trees had been blown down crisscross. My curiosity was piqued by the queer-looking affair and I climbed along one of the tree trunks to see what it was. Suddenly, as I got almost over it, the whole mass began to shake and quiver and out came an old Black Bear and two cubs. This was the only time that I ever actually knew of a Black Bear and her cubs having denned up together. And I have never seen more than a dozen cases where it seemed probable that they had. Later on on this same trip I saw seven other Black Bear sleeping places, all in similar situations under tree trunks or tangled down-timber.

Only a year ago, up at Priest Lake, in Idaho, some

friends and myself came across the tracks of a cougar, and, having gone back for dogs, we returned and put them on its trail. We were in full chase along the side of a mountain when one of the dogs attracted my attention by the way he acted. He turned aside, rushed to a dead tree that lay along the ground, and began excitedly sniffing at one end of it. I knew that the cougar could not be there and went over to see what was attracting the dog's attention, and saw instantly that a Black Bear had been denned up under the log, but, disturbed by the dog's approach, had broken out and made off down the mountain in a foot and a half of snow.

These are merely examples of many such experiences, and I have more than once followed the trail of a bear and seen where it had made itself a new retreat.

We know, since they lay up no store of provisions, that the bear does not eat during its long retirement, and although, in the north, it would be possible for it to provide itself with water by eating the snow that shuts it in, we know that bears hibernating in captivity (a thing by the way that they do not often do) neither eat nor drink.

One odd fact about the whole proceeding is that all bears of the same class in the same locality go into winter quarters and emerge from them within a few days of each other. In the Selkirk Mountains in British Columbia, I have seen where six grizzlies had broken their way through several feet of snow out of six different caves on the side of a single mountain all in one night. In localities where both species are found, the Black Bear come out from one to two months earlier than the grizzlies, and in both species the males emerge two weeks or more before the females with new cubs. But all of each kind come out within a day or two of each other.

I incline to the belief that in the majority of cases the Black Bear, when in freedom, breeds every year. Most authorities on bears who base their opinions upon observations made on captive animals, claim that both the grizzly and the Black Bear breed annually. But a long series of observations and the closest possible attention given to this point has absolutely convinced me that it is the very rare exception when a free female grizzly breeds oftener than once in two years. I have seen many hundreds of grizzly mothers with cubs in the open, and fully as many of them were followed by yearling cubs as by spring cubs. But although (the Black Bear being much more numerous than the grizzly) I have seen many more Black Bears with cubs than grizzlies with cubs, I have never seen more than a dozen Black Bear mothers followed by yearling cubs.

I have therefore been forced to conclude that it is the habit of the Black Bear to wean its cubs and abandon them before denning up the first fall. In the case of the grizzly the mother and the cubs den up together the fall following the latter's birth, and run together during the following summer, and it is not until late in the second season that the mother turns the cubs adrift to shift for themselves. This family of young grizzlies then usually den up together and continue to run together the third summer, at the close of which the litter disbands and the individuals belonging to it take up their separate lives. I have also seen a few litters of yearling Black Bears still running in company without their mother; but as this is by no means a common sight, I believe that ordinarily Black Bear cubs den up separately after they leave their mother at the close of their first summer.

Inasmuch, however, as I have seen a few Black Bear mothers followed by yearling cubs, I assume that in these cases the mother and cubs had denned up together in the same manner that the grizzlies habitually do. And I once actually found an old Black Bear and two cubs so settled for the winter. I have also tracked an old grizzly and her cubs to where they had gone into winter quarters together, and have seen where a grizzly mother and her year-old family had emerged from hibernation in company the second spring. I have also often seen where a litter of two-year-old grizzly cubs had wintered together in one cave after leaving their mother in their third fall, but I have never seen any actual evidence of young Black Bears wintering together in this manner.

I believe that the explanation of this very striking difference of habit between the Black and the grizzly bears in the matter of breeding annually or biennially, is to be found in their different degrees of fierceness, and in the resulting fact that the Black Bear cubs are not so long in danger from the evil tempers and bloodthirsty dispositions of the grown males of their kind.

A new-born cub of either species would be instantly killed, and probably eaten, by any old male that got the opportunity; and, unnatural as this seems to us, it is true of many or most carnivorous, or partly carnivorous, animals. It is true of rats, as most boys who have bred white rats have had occasion to discover. The memory of the habit, at least, survives in the fierceness with which even a pet dog with puppies will keep the father of them away from her basket. In all zoological gardens it is necessary to separate the male bears from the female at and after the birth of cubs, and the habits of mother bears in the woods show that their instincts warn them very effectually of the wisdom of this course.

But while the Black Bear mother shows no great concern for the safety of her cubs after they have reached the age of five or six months, the grizzly mother continues, with good reason, to evade or resent the approach of other members of her tribe till well into the second year. I have on two different occasions known of a male grizzly's killing and eating a cub that had been left fastened by a chain near a camp; and in one instance I came upon a grizzly that had just killed a female and had eaten her two cubs. She had been caught in a steel trap set by a trapper, and her two cubs were with her. The male, finding her in this predicament, had doubtless attacked the cubs, and when, hampered as she was by the trap and clog, she had attempted to defend them, he had killed her too.

A female grizzly with young is one of the most dangerous animals in the world. She will allow no other bear of either sex to approach either her or them. And this invariable attitude of her fully accounts, to my mind, for her failure to breed while the young are still with her. But the Black Bear mother is not only a comparatively inoffensive animal at all times, but she seems to have no such lasting distrust of other members of her own species. I have often seen an old Black Bear asleep in the branches of a tree with her five or six-months-old cubs frisking around on the ground, when she must have been well aware that there were Black Bears of the opposite sex in the neighborhood. This is not to be put down to indifference on her part. It simply means that the necessity for watchfulness has passed. It therefore becomes easily understandable that the Black Bear mother can afford, without risk to her half-grown cubs, to breed every year in the open; while the grizzly does not, until her young are fully able to take care of themselves unaided, dare to associate with their possible enemies—the cantankerous males of the tribe.

The records of the Lodges contain one or two interesting notes relating to these matters. The first time that their original pair of Black Bears bred they did not separate the mother and father, and the first intimation that they had of the birth of cubs was the appearance of the father at the mouth of the den with a dead cub in its mouth. After that they took care to give the female separate quarters. Again, the only two occasions during the last sixteen or eighteen years on which this female has failed to breed have been in years when her cubs were allowed to remain with her throughout the summer, and when, as the owners state, she was so taken up with them that she refused to have anything to do with her mate.

This is exactly the attitude that my observations have led me to assume as habitual on the part of the free grizzly. And I imagine that the Black Bear mother adopted it in this case because, in the narrow quarters of a twenty-foot bear-pit, she was afraid to relax her vigilance, as she doubtless would have felt justified in doing in her natural surroundings.

Another point of difference between the two species that agrees with the earlier abandonment of its young by the Black Bear is the fact that these appear to breed at least a year earlier than the young of the grizzly. The latter, as we have seen, only separate

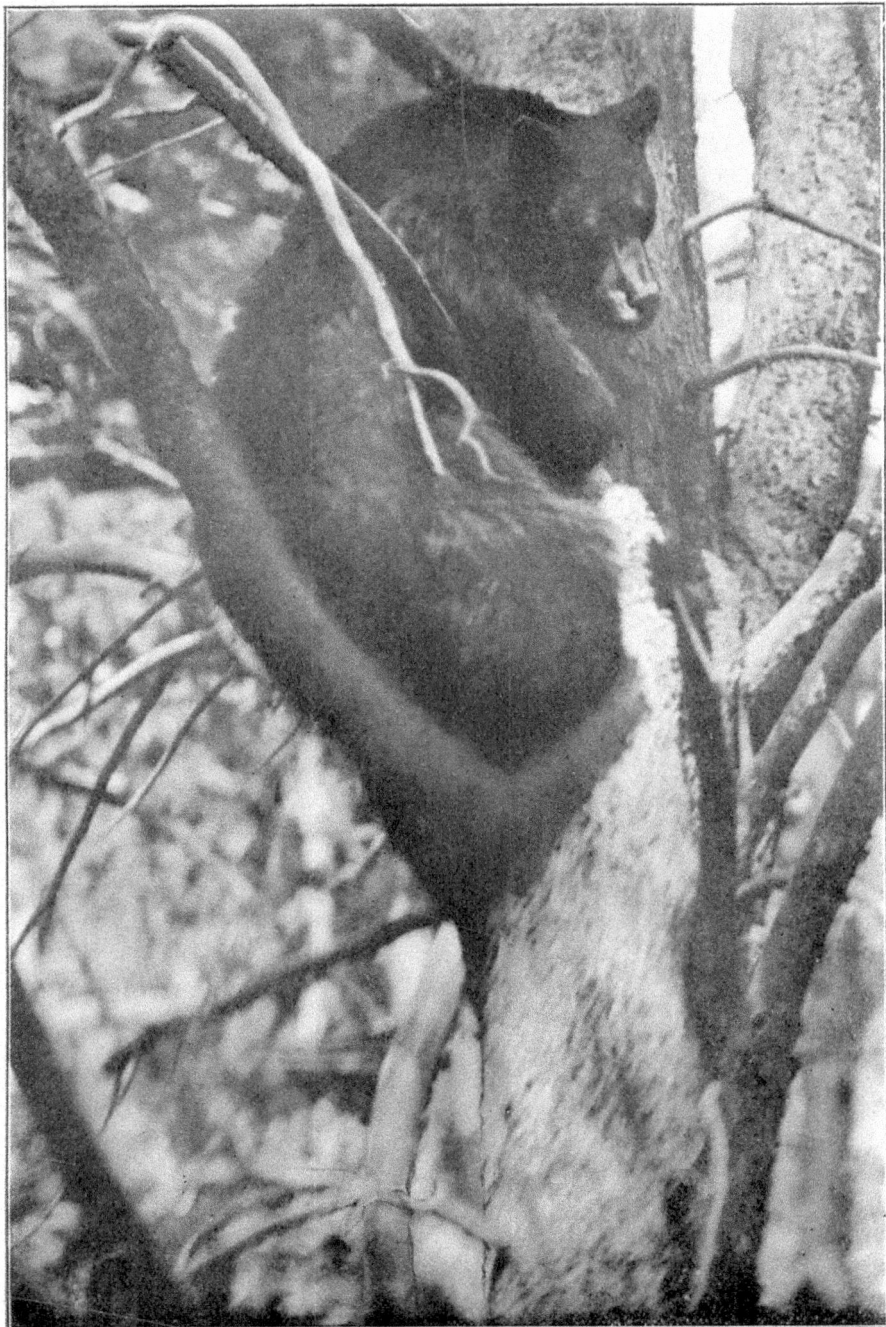

Taking a sun bath

and den up individually at the end of their third summer and breed the following year at the earliest; but I have seen Black Bear mothers that could not have weighed over a hundred pounds, and that made the most amusing and appealing picture of youthful responsibility.

There is a widespread notion that bears are given to travelling in company; that they are sociable animals, and that bear families—father, mother, and children—are not only to be met with in the woods, but den up together for the winter. This is not true. Only mothers and cubs or occasionally half-grown cubs of one litter ever travel together. I have never seen the slightest evidence that grown bears, male and female, ever travel in couples, even in the mating season; and I have never known a case where full-grown animals of any bear species denned up together. These statements apply no less to the Black Bear than to the grizzly.

Another point on which there is much popular misconception and disbelief is the extreme smallness of bear cubs at birth. This, at first glance, is not only astonishing, but to many people seems almost incredible. "How is it possible," they ask, "and why is it advantageous for an animal as large as a bear to have young so small? Why, the puppies of a forty-pound dog are as large as the cubs of the four-hundred pound bear!" Yet the fact remains, and in the case of the grizzly, where the mother sometimes weighs twice as much as the Black Bear mother, the cubs are, if anything, a trifle smaller at birth on the average. I have never heard the matter explained, but it seems to me that when we consider the yearly habits of the bear they tend to suggest how this peculiar race-habit was developed. A dog mother with three or four puppies, weighing six or eight ounces apiece at birth, will eat three huge meals a day and grow thin as a rail nursing her hungry youngsters. What, then, would become of a bear mother who had to nurse three or four cubs for six weeks or two months, with never a meal at all, if the cubs were born weighing five or six pounds? It looks very much as though Nature, with her usual skill at making both ends meet, had so arranged matters in the bear family that, as these animals developed the hibernating habit, the size of the cubs was reduced in proportion to the reduced ability of the mother to nourish them. And that three or four eight-ounce cubs do not make any undue demands on the resources of a three-hundred or four-hundred-pound mother is proved by the fact that both she and they are normally in excellent condition when they first come out in the spring.

FOOD AND FEEDING

THE Black Bear is described as omnivorous. Literally, that means that he eats everything; and this comes pretty near to being literally true, for he has democratic tastes, a magnificent appetite, and nothing much to do between meals. Technically, however, the term means that the Black Bear is both carnivorous and herbivorous; that he eats flesh like a wolf, grass like an ox, fish like an otter, carrion like a coyote, bugs like a hen, and berries like a bird. In short he eats pretty much everything he can get, and pretty generally all he can get of it.

One would naturally imagine that so thorough-going a feeder would emerge from his long and complete winter fast ravenously hungry and ready to fall tooth and claw upon a hearty breakfast. But this is not so. Indeed, when we stop to think of it, we can see that even a bear's cast-iron constitution and digestive apparatus would hardly stand such treatment. I have examined the stomach and intestines of a bear killed just as it came out in the spring, and not only found them utterly empty, but flattened with disuse. These organs have, therefore, to be treated with consideration and coaxed back gradually to the performance of their accustomed functions. Shipwrecked sailors, rescued at the point of starvation, have to be forced by their friends to go slowly until their stomachs again get the habit of digestion; and while bears have no friends to do them a like service, they have practised long fasting for so many generations that they have developed instincts that serve the purpose.

When they first come out of the winter's den they wander around for a day or so showing little or no inclination for food. Then they make their way down to where the snow is gone and the early vegetation has begun to sprout, and eat sparingly of the tender grass shoots. But their appetites are not long in returning. By the end of a week the old saying, "hungry as a bear," is more than justified and they start in in earnest to make up for lost time. At this season they are especially fond of the parsnip-like roots of the skunk cabbage, and I have seen marshy bottom lands so dug over by bears in search of this dainty that they had almost the appearance of having been ploughed.

Here again the experience of the Lodges with their captive bears exactly confirms my own observations in the open. Mr. William R. Lodge writes me that, "When they first come out they are not hungry, and the first day or two only partake of a bite or two of parsnip or similar food that we always provide and that seems to be their most satisfactory diet after they acquire the habit of eating again." Later on these Cuyahoga Falls animals are given young dandelion leaves, clover, scraps from the hotel tables, berries, watermelons, sweet corn, and acorns. I have no doubt that this diet, so carefully approximated to the natural food of the animal in its free state, has had much to do with the success of the owners in inducing them to breed.

Wild white clover is another favorite dish of the Black Bear, and they eat the buds of the young maple shrubs and other tender green stuff. They do not, however, do nearly so much digging as the grizzly. I have seen acres of stony ground literally spaded up by the latter in search of the bulbs of the dog-tooth violet and the spring beauty. But it is only here and there, where a thin layer of earth covers a smooth hillside or ledge of rock and supports a meagre crop of small roots, that the Black Bear will scoop these up and eat them; and apart from the easy work of turning over the soft swamp earth for skunk-cabbage roots they are little given to such systematic labor.

Here indeed one sees one of the most striking differences of habit and disposition between the Black Bear and the grizzly. The grizzlies work for their food like industrious men. The Black Bear will work hard at any kind of mischief, but seems to hate to work steadily for business purposes. The grizzly will dig for hours and heap out cartloads of earth and rock to get at a nest of marmots or ground-squirrels. The Black Bear may show an interest in a marmot burrow and do a little half-hearted scratching near the entrance, but never digs deep or long for them. As far as I have ever seen, they kill nothing larger, in the way of small game, than field-mice and such small fry. But they are both quick and clever at catching these. They will turn over stumps and roll logs aside and up-end flat stones and catch an escaping mouse before it goes a yard.

Frogs and toads are also favorite tidbits of theirs and they spend much time looking for them. They will walk along the edge of small streams and pin down a jumping frog with their lightning-quick paws; and I have seen one, when a frog escaped it and jumped into the creek, jump after it and land like a stone from a catapult, splashing water for twenty feet.

Practically nothing in the insect line comes amiss to them. They are everlastingly poking and pulling at rotten logs, old stumps, loose stones, and decaying trees, looking for caterpillars, squash-bugs, grubs, centipedes, and larvæ. Their sense of smell is wonderfully acute and one can hear them sniffing and snuffing over the punky mass of an old tree trunk they have ripped open, searching with their noses for crawling goodies.

Like all bears they are extravagantly fond of ants, and they are not only experts in finding them, but know how to take advantage of the habits of the various kinds in order to catch them. Their greatest feasts in this line are obtained when they discover the huge low hills of what, in the West, are called Vinegar Ants. These are only moderate in size, but are extremely vicious. They get their name from a strong odor, resembling that of vinegar, that they exhale when aroused. They build large hills, sometimes several feet in diameter, made up for the most part of pine needles, bits of wood, pellets of earth, and such like stuff. They are red and black in color, have powerful jaws, and rush by the thousand to give battle to any intruder that disturbs their home. It is this latter trait that makes them an easy prey to the Black Bear. When he discovers an ant-hill belonging to this species he walks up to it, runs one of his fore-legs deep down into the inside of it, gives a turn to his paw that effectually stirs things up below, and then stretches himself out at ease to await results, with his front legs extended to the base of the hill.

Out rush the ants by companies and regiments and brigades; mad as hornets, brave as lions, smelling like a spoiled vinegar mill, and looking for trouble. They get it, almost immediately. They discover the bear's furry paws and, struggling and tumbling in the hair like angry and hurrying warriors in a jungle, they begin to swarm over them. And as fast as they come the bear licks them up. When the excitement dies down, he gives the inside of the hill another poke. This results in another sortie of defenders, and when these have stormed the hairy heights and been eaten for their pains, he repeats the operation. I believe a bear would eat a solid bushel of these insects at a sitting. On the other hand, a bear will by no means despise a single ant, and one of the best ways of making friends with a young cub is to catch a stray ant and offer it to him. He will lean forward, sniff at your fingers, and then grab the dainty as eagerly as though it weighed a pound.

There is another variety of ants, larger than the so-called Vinegar Ants, which are black and live, for the most part, under flat rocks. These the bear will lap up with his tongue after uncovering their retreat. And there is still another variety of huge black ants that nest about the roots of trees and spend their time exploring the bark and branches. I have seen them sixty feet above ground busily pursuing their affairs. Of these, too, the Black Bear is fond, and one sees him snuffing and smelling around the cracks in old trees in hopes of locating a colony of them. I have seen where bears have scratched and gnawed at the edges of a narrow opening in the lower trunk of a decaying tree, in a vain endeavor to get into the open heart of it; and again, where they had ripped off a rotting slab and gained a feast. For in cold weather these ants gather in sluggish masses and later even freeze solid—I have seen what would make a quart of them so frozen—and seem to take no harm from the cold storage. By the way, the bear is not alone in liking this peculiar diet. I have seen French Canadian lumber jacks pick up handfuls of these frozen black ants and eat them. One of them once informed me that they tasted "just the same like raspberries."

The Black Bear is also fond of bumble-bees, yellow-jackets, wasps, and hornets. He is the bear that is, when occasion offers, the honey-eater; but in the Rockies and Western coast ranges there are few wild honey-bees, and so his taste in that direction is seldom indulged, but he makes up for this by hunting out and eating such bees as he can find. He will dig up bumble-bees and eat them and will lap yellow-jackets off his fur exactly as he does ants. Of course the bear is fully protected by his thick coat from any attack by the bees, and if the latter sting his mouth or tongue as he swallows them, he manages to disguise the fact very thoroughly. I have never seen one shake his head or otherwise advertise a mishap of this kind.

But all these bugs and bees and ants and mice are, after all, but the luxuries and dessert of the Black Bear's diet. He is, for the most part, a vegetarian, does far more grazing than is ordinarily supposed, and has his real season of plenty and stuffing when the berry season arrives. He will travel miles to get to a berry patch, and even when tamed and half domesti-cated will often try to escape to the open for this annual feast. A chain that has proved amply strong enough to hold a Black Bear captive during the spring and early summer is very likely to turn up broken when the blueberries ripen. Their favorites everywhere are blueberries and huckleberries, and the black and red haws, called thorn-apples in New England. The sarvis berry is another of their staples. They will reach up one paw, draw down a laden berry bush, and grasping it between their forefeet will rake the fruit into their open mouths. But the Black Bear is less particular in regard to berries than the grizzly. He will eat pretty much anything in that line, even feeding on the Oregon grape in the Rockies, a food disdained by the grizzly.

In the East they also feed greedily on acorns and beechnuts, and in the West they eat the seeds that drop out of the pine cones. In the higher ranges of the Tetons and Bitter Roots, and indeed throughout the Rockies down into Mexico, there is a tree locally called the Jack Pine that bears a curious cone two or three inches across the butt and only two or three inches in depth —as broad as it is long, in fact. These cones contain very large and meaty seeds and the Black Bear is very fond of them. The Indians also cook and eat the young cones of the Jack Pine.

In addition to this the Black Bear has a great habit of peeling the bark off of balsam and of Jack Pine saplings, and of lapping the juices and gum from the wounds. They also scrape the gummy pulp from the inside of the bark and eat it. The grizzly never does these things. This pulp, however, is used by some of the Indians, who make a kind of bread out of it.

The Black Bear is fond of fish, but here again shows himself less clever and less industrious than the grizzly, who is an expert fisherman. On the Pacific slope of the Rocky Mountains almost every stream has, or used to have, its runs of salmon, these fish making their way to the upper reaches of the smaller rivers for the purpose of spawning. There are several varieties of these fish, and they enter the river and start on their long, up-hill journeys at different seasons. But one and all they are moved by a single desire—to get as far up stream as it is possible to go; and are driven forward by so strong an instinct that neither wounds, nor weariness, nor exhaustion, nor the fear of death itself, deters them from attempting (and sometimes accomplishing) what seems like the impossible.

They come from undiscovered regions of the sea in uncountable billions. In untold millions they enter the mouths of the great rivers. They turn off into each tributary stream by hundreds of thousands. They fill the tributaries of these tributaries. And finally one finds them, still in their hundreds, filling the pools of the smaller rivers, leaping, floundering, all but crawling through the riffles and shallows of the smaller creeks, thousands of feet above the sea, and still undaunted.

And few of the invading millions ever find their way back to the ocean from which they came. From the moment that they enter the mouths of the larger rivers, every living creature, from man downward, begins to take toll of them. Those that pass the nets and salmon wheels of the canning factories, that elude the talons of the eagles and ospreys, that are missed by the paws of the bears and the cougars, the teeth of the otters and the mink, arrive at the head-waters of their selected stream in a pitiable condition of wounds and exhaustion. Their fins are nothing but bare spines. Their sides are torn by rocks, they are thin from fasting, and when they have deposited and fertilized the eggs that they have come so far to find fit hatcheries for, they are, for the most part, utterly unable to manage the long return journey. Then they fall an easy prey to any animal that finds them. And many animals gather to the feast. Here is the free-lunch counter of the wilderness; during the salmon runs everything in the mountains lives on fish: bears, cougars, coyotes, wolverines, lynx; in Alaska the very geese gorge themselves on salmon; and the Black Bear gets his share of the loot.

The grizzly, as I have said, is an expert fisherman. I have seen one toss out seventeen big salmon in less than an hour, and after eating his fill bury the rest of his catch for future use. But the Black Bears only fish on their own account occasionally and in very shallow water. They will wander along the trails on the banks of the small streams, and if salmon are struggling over the riffles, will jump in and catch one or two. But they are too much lacking in patience to wait for the fish as the grizzly does, and too improvident to do more than supply the need of the moment when the opportunity comes unwaited for. And they are quite satisfied, for the most part, to take the leavings of others or to feed on stranded or dead fish. They often get crumbs from the table of the golden eagle, the bald eagle, and the osprey; and sometimes, when one of these birds catches a fish too heavy to fly away with, a Black Bear will drive the fisherman away and eat his catch for him.

But we began by saying that the Black Bear was in part carnivorous, and so far, we have not justified the claim by anything more fleshy than a field-mouse. The truth is that the Black Bear much prefers to have his meat "well hung," as some sportsmen express it. That is to say, he really prefers carrion. Any kind of a carcass makes a strong appeal to him, and I do not believe that meat can be too putrid to suit his taste. Ben, when he was out walking with me during the time we lived in Missoula, would turn aside to sniff over any dead cat or hen that he came across—even if nothing remained of it but dried skin and bones.

And he would actually lie down and roll on the find, and, if allowed, would then pick it up in his mouth and carry it home for a nest egg.

But in spite of his preference for carrion, the Black Bear soon learns to take advantage of easily procurable live meat. They are remarkably adaptable animals, take kindly to civilization, and accommodate themselves readily to the conditions and opportunities that follow in its wake. They very soon realize it if they are free from interference, and will, with the slightest encouragement, begin to impose upon you. They will live under your barn with the best will in the world. And they'll learn to steal sheep. In some localities they get to be a serious nuisance in this way. But their favorite civilized dish is young pig. In some regions the ranchmen in the spring turn their hogs out into swamps to feed on the roots of the skunk cabbage; but if Black Bears happen to be plentiful in the neighborhood they are very likely to get not only the skunk cabbage but the pigs as well. There appears to be something about a shoat that appeals directly to the Black Bear instinct. They learn to be sheep thieves; but they appear to be born pig thieves. The summer that I caught Ben, as we were returning to Spokane across the Palouse farming country, we stopped at a ranch over night and left Ben tied under a small shed while we unpacked and stabled our horses. It happened that there was an old sow with a litter of young pigs in a pen at the rear end of the shed, and that there was a hole in the pen for the young ones to come and go by. And when we came back to get Ben we found him lying by this hole with one paw stuck through it, waiting for a pig. And just as we arrived he actually slapped one on the nose and almost caught it. And he was only a little larger than the pig himself.

Of course the diet of the Black Bear, like that of the grizzly, and of most other wild animals, depends largely upon the locality in which they live. There are regions where, of necessity, the bear are largely if not altogether vegetarians; and others where, at certain seasons, they live almost wholly upon fish or largely upon carrion. It is never safe to generalize from localized observations as to the food habits of any animal, and it is only very carefully and as the result of a broad experience that one should venture to ascribe to any species the traits that one has observed in individuals. There is one feeding habit of the Black Bear, however, that I believe to be universally typical. They never make caches of food. The grizzlies will, as I have already said, bury the fish they cannot eat for future use. They will also drag away and bury or hide the carcass of any animal they have found and will return to feed on it until it is all consumed; or they will carefully cover it where it lies with earth and leaves and branches to prevent other animals from finding it in their absence. The Black Bear does not look so far ahead. He will carry away a few pounds of meat or bones in his mouth, but beyond that appears to take no thought for the morrow. When he has sated his appetite on a carcass he will leave it where and as he found it. He lives from hand to mouth and is the Happy Hooligan of the woods.

THE HAPPY HOOLIGAN

In this chapter I would like to give some notion of the Black Bear at home. I do not mean "at home" in the society sense of being dressed up "from four to seven" to receive callers; but in the good old backwoods sense of being in your shirt-sleeves with your feet on the table. There is a good deal more difference between the two attitudes than appears in a book on etiquette.

If you meet a man at an afternoon reception you see one side of him—the outside. If you are a member of the local vigilance committee and call on him officially in the course of business, you get a specialized insight into another phase of his character. But as an old hermit with a rat-tailed file for a tongue once said to me in the hills, "You never really know a man till you've watched him through the transom when he thinks himself alone."

It is pretty much the same with bears. We are all familiar with them as seen at their public receptions in the bear pits. We know their company manners. Personally, I can never quite rid myself of the absurd notion that when the guards put the crowds out at five o'clock and close the Zoo gates for the night, the bears must yawn, stretch their cramped muscles, shake themselves with that lumbering, disjointed violence of theirs, and exclaim in bear language, "Thank heaven, *that's* over until to-morrow!"

For the rest most of our information about them comes from self-appointed vigilantes who, rifle in hand, knock unexpectedly at the doors of their summer residences and do not even offer them the customary five minutes in which to say their prayers. In their reports, as in accounts of other executions, the chief emphasis is laid upon the attitude of the victim in the face of death. "The condemned mounted the steps of the scaffold with a firm tread." Or, if the animal happened to be gnawing a bone when discovered, "At the conclusion of a hearty breakfast consisting of ham and eggs and coffee, the sheriff came in and read the death-warrant." Or, best of all, if the unhappy brute ventured to show its teeth as the firing squad sighted down the rifle barrel, we are informed that, "the savage and bloodthirsty monster died game."

This may be good journalism, but it is mighty poor natural history. It gives us some insight into the nature of the man behind the gun, but very little idea of the real nature of the bear in front of it. We never find out what the bear would have done if the trigger had not been pulled. A man once stopped before a plant in my garden and asked me what under the shin-

She began to swing her head from side to side

ing sun it was. He had never, he said, seen anything like it. As a matter of fact it happened to be a cabbage that had gone to seed; but the man, who had always killed his cabbages as soon as their hides were prime, did not even know they bore seed. And he rather fancied himself as an amateur gardener, too. It is much the same in the woods. If you kill your bear just as soon as it begins to act natural, you may get to be an authority on hides, but there will be a lot of things that you don't know.

We are not here discussing the ethics of killing. That is a question quite apart. Goodness knows that there is little enough glory—since there is little or no risk—in killing a Black Bear. To chase a timorous and inoffensive animal up a tree and then to stand underneath and shoot it is no very great achievement. The sport is altogether in the mind of the sportsman. It is a good deal like dressing up in a brown cotton imitation of a fringed buckskin hunting shirt and stalking the spring calf in the east pasture with an airgun. It's exciting—until you find out what it really amounts to. But you have to manufacture your own excitement. The point I wish to make is simply this: that if you want to find out how an animal lives, you must watch it live and not watch it die. When you start out to study the habits of a wild animal the place for your gun, if you have one, is in the rack at home.

For one thing, if you undertake to watch a man

through a transom with a gun in your hand and murder in your mind, the chances are a hundred to one that he'll feel something queer "in the air." The thing has not been explained yet, but we can feel a scowl behind our backs much more readily than a smile. And in the woods the animals soon distinguish between a desire to kill and a desire to look on. I have tried both and I know.

All animals are quick to understand when we are afraid of them; and many of them seem to enjoy taking advantage of the fact. We can see this in cows and in dogs and even in turkey gobblers. And we would see it often in the woods, too, if we were not so much given to either running or shooting before we had time to see it. The Black Bear makes the most of his ability to inspire terror. He trades on it. He makes capital out of it. And he has come to be one of the most accomplished bluffers on earth.

In the summer of 1908 I spent some weeks in the mountains of the Yellowstone National Park getting a series of flash-light pictures of grizzly bears, and early in my stay I was joined by Mr. J. B. Kerfoot, of New York, who, although he had had no experience with bears, had done a good deal of amateur photography and was anxious to help me with the work in hand. The day after we reached camp we went out to look over the ground where we proposed to work that night, and on our way back we ran across an old Black Bear with two cubs and determined to take her picture. As soon as she saw us she ordered her cubs up a tree but, by a quick movement, I managed to get to them in time to intercept the second cub before it had a chance to obey. It then rejoined its mother and I placed myself between them and the treed cub and thus had things just as I wanted them, knowing that the old bear would not go far away and leave her youngster (who was bawling lustily from the branches) to its possible fate.

But when I called Kerfoot, who had the camera, to come forward and get some pictures, he was rather shy about it. He explained that he had come out to photograph bears, and that if this one had been by herself, he would not have minded her; but that he had always understood that an old bear with cubs was about the most dangerous thing on four legs, and that to interpose himself between her and her bawling off-spring looked to him a good deal like suicide. I finally persuaded him that there was no danger, however, and he moved up to within fifty feet or so of the old bear. But he had no more than taken a step or two when she turned toward him with a coughing snarl that made him think his last hour had come. I could not help laughing at the old bluffer, for she had never so much as shown me a tooth, but had rather assumed toward me what you might call a "put upon" expression— whining and walking nervously back and forth and

showing quite plainly that she thought herself badly
used by a superior force.   But Kerfoot was hard to con-
vince in regard to her bluffing qualities, and while we
were all manœuvring for a suitable position the cub
came down from the tree, joined its mother and the
other cub, and all three made off into the woods.

We followed helter-skelter, and as the cubs could not
run very fast we finally succeeded in treeing one of them
again and resumed operations.   This time I picked up
a club and by brandishing it valiantly every time the
bear snarled at Kerfoot, managed to reassure him
sufficiently to coax him up within about thirty feet of
her.   He had a Graflex natural-history camera that
took a 4 × 5 plate, but had sufficient bellows to accommodate a twenty-inch lens, thus giving a very large
image at a comparatively considerable distance from
the object.   In these cameras an inclined mirror, that
flies out of the way at the moment of exposure, enables
one to see the full-sized picture on the ground glass,
and to focus on a moving subject up to the second of
pressing the button.   And when Kerfoot had looked
at the picture at a distance of thirty feet he said that
he thought he could get a fine head by going a bit
closer yet, and moved ten feet nearer.   He had just
gotten things to his liking and was standing with the
long camera held at the level of his eye and his head
bent over the focussing hood when the bear gave a
vicious snort, and executed the peculiar combination

of broken coughs and gnashing teeth that is the trump card in the Black Bear's game of bluff; and the photographer literally went straight up into the air. Of course the whole effect was reproduced on the ground glass within two inches of his eyes and he said afterward that he had thought his nose was scratched. But the sight was too much for me. I threw away my club, and throwing myself on the ground roared with laughter, and as soon as he understood what had happened, Kerfoot put the camera down and joined me.

And when we had laughed ourselves almost into tears we found the old bear sitting on her haunches and looking at us as serious as an owl. That ended her bluffing and we got several pictures of her, one of which, taken just before we left her, is reproduced here. By that time the poor old soul had so worried herself over the other cub that she was literally drenched in sweat, and she finally sat down and began to swing her head dejectedly from side to side, uttering a sort of moan at each swing, for all the world like a mourner at a wake, while the cub that was with her sat back and looked on. It was at this moment that the picture was taken, and when we had secured it we were so sorry for her that we packed up and left her alone.

This experience gave Mr. Kerfoot a pretty good insight into the real meaning of Black Bear ferocity, and later on we had many amusing experiences with the beasts. To show, however, that some people have eyes but do not use them, I will give another little adventure that we had toward the end of our stay in the mountain. We had with us as camp keeper a man who has lived most of his life in the Rockies, has hunted bears all over that part of the country, and ought to have been pretty well acquainted with the real nature of them. I do not believe that with a gun in his hand he would be afraid of anything that walks, but he had evidently never investigated very closely into what would happen to him when he had left his gun at home. We had stopped over night at a public camp at a place called Tower Falls, and after supper in the evening Kerfoot and I, having seen a Black Bear at the edge of a clearing, walked over to look at her. She was a large animal and lay on the ground near the foot of a big pine tree, and a single cub sat on one of the low-hanging branches above her head. We were talking about our plans for the morrow and walked toward the bear without thinking much about her one way or the other. When we got within fifty feet or so of her she backed up against the tree, and as we continued to advance without noticing her especially, she first stood up with her feet against the trunk and then climbed up ten or fifteen feet from the ground, driving her cub ahead of her. We walked up to the foot of the tree and looked at her for a few minutes, and though she stuck her upper lip out at us in the peculiar fashion of her kind, she made no other demonstration, and after we had stood there and talked for a little while, we turned back toward camp.

About half-way back we met our man Frank coming down to see the bear, and just behind him came a party of eight or ten people who had stopped for the night at the camp. We paid no attention to this crowd until, hearing a noise behind us, we turned around and found the whole lot running back up the hill very much frightened, and as Frank was bringing up the rear we asked him, rather jokingly, what was the matter. "Gee," he answered, "I tell you, that's a fierce old bear." And we have not finished teasing him about it yet. That old bear certainly knew whom to bluff, and I have no doubt that the majority of the school-teachers in the crowd thought themselves lucky to have escaped with their heads.

I do not mean to say that a Black Bear will not fight if it is forced to. But, personally, I have never seen one's patience tried to the breaking point. If you chase one too closely it will take to a tree. If you follow it up the trunk, it will retreat toward the top. I imagine that if you kept on following it until it could go no farther you would end up by getting a pretty bad mauling, for it has sharp claws and tremendous muscles to back them up with; but it is perfectly safe to say that if you were at the top of the tree and it was half-way down, you would have a hard time getting at close enough quarters with it to get hurt.

These conclusions, like all the others scattered through the pages of this book, are founded upon many observations made during many years, not upon any single experience or upon the actions of any one animal; and I want to lay especial emphasis upon the fact that when I give, as an illustration, the account of any particular happening, it is only cited as an example of the things that, taken together, have gone to the forming of my belief.   For instance, in the summer of 1906 I was camped high up on the continental divide in the mountains of Wyoming with two boys, Tommy and Bill Richards.   One day when we were out in the hills we saw a Black Bear go into a thick tangle of underbrush surrounding a big pine tree and lying at the foot of a perpendicular cliff; and we determined for the fun of the thing to drive it out so as to get a good look at it.   I accordingly made my way to the extreme right of the thicket, Bill stationed himself in front, and Tommy stayed where we were when we first saw the bear.   Then at a given signal we all rushed in with loud yells.   But instead of trying to escape, the bear went up the pine tree and lodged thirty feet or so from the ground in a clump of foliage. One of the boys had a camera and now wanted to get the bear's picture, so I suggested that he could do this by driving the bear further up the tree, and as Tommy said he was not afraid of the animal I cut him a long pole and he climbed up to where he could reach up and

A black bear at home

poke the bear with it. He punched it in the belly and the bear was furious, slashed at the stick, gnashed its teeth, and made a most terrifying fuss, but refused to move. Tommy, however, kept on poking and in a few minutes the bear got over its anger, appeared to grow interested in the game, and before they got through, it was actually *playing*. Tommy took to tickling its feet, and it would raise first one and then the other and try to catch the pole with its teeth and claws, all in a high good humor. Tommy finally dislodged him by climbing higher yet and fairly threshing the branches with his pole, and they got an excellent photograph that they subsequently published in the *St. Nicholas* magazine.

The Black Bear is very fond of water, and seldom stays for any length of time where it cannot get its daily bath. The grizzly also bathes, especially in hot weather or to rid itself of vermin, but the Black Bear loves water for its own sake. They have regular bathing holes and after taking a swim either stretch themselves out on a grassy bed near by, or climb up into a convenient tree, where the sun and wind soon dries them off. We found one such bear's bath tub in a beautifully situated glade among the mountains and spent a good deal of time concealed in some nearby shrubbery, hoping to get a picture of Ursus emerging from the bath. During one of these waits a small Black Bear sauntered up to the edge of the pool, looked carefully around as though to make sure he was alone, and then slipped into the water and swam twice the length of the plunge.   Just as he was crawling out on to the bank again, Kerfoot snapped his camera at him and, frightened by the sound, the bear took to his heels and climbed up a near-by tree.   He settled himself about forty feet from the ground in the sunlight, and having apparently made up his mind that he had been scared over nothing settled down for a comfortable snooze. We now made up our minds that we would like a second picture to complete our record of the performance, and walked over to the bottom of the tree where the bear was ensconced, but, as is usually the case with these black animals, we found that the position in which he sat did not lend itself to a picture, so we sat down under the tree determined to wait till he changed his position.   Nothing happened for fifteen or twenty minutes, when, quite unexpectedly, the bear made up his mind that he was not going to be held prisoner any longer, and with a great puffing and snorting, started stern first down the tree.   Kerfoot, who by this time had gotten over his initial ideas about Black Bear, picked up a stick and hammered on the trunk to scare him back again.   But this was one of the bears who, when he bluffed, bluffed to the limit, and, instead of retreating, he redoubled his growls and snarls and continued to come steadily down the tree.   By this time I was becoming interested and was making bets with myself as to which of the two bluffers (for I knew that they were both bluffing) would eventually take the trick. Kerfoot finally settled the matter by actually hitting the bear a whack over the rump with his club, and the latter scurried back up the tree, twice as fast as he had come down.

One of the most characteristic features of the Black Bear's game of bluff is its utter failure to show any concern when the bluff is called. A dog, for instance, when he indulges in a bluff that fails to work, very frequently shows plainly that he feels himself a fool. He'll rush out with every evidence of intending to attack; growling, snarling, and coming headlong toward you; and when (if you know dogs and are not impressed by his fine acting) he gets quite up to you without frightening you, he will cringe, lick your boots, sometimes roll over and put all four feet up—which is the dog sign of complete discomfiture or complete surrender. Of course it is not possible for us to really know how any animal's mind works. We are almost certain to credit them with some of our own psychology in trying to follow theirs. And so I do not mean to imply that a dog under these circumstances "thinks he is a fool." But we know that he acts very much as we would feel if we thought we had been shown up. The nearest that we can come to interpreting his actions is to say that they seem to mean, "I did not know that it was *you*, or I never would have tried to frighten you."

But a Black Bear does not, as the boys say, give a continental whether his bluff works or not. If he scares you, well and good. He's gained his point. If he doesn't scare you, well and good again. Nothing has been lost by the attempt. In ninety-nine cases out of a hundred he'll sit and look at you exactly as though nothing had happened, and the inference is, "Well, *I've* made *my* suggestion. Now it's *your* move." It was thoroughly typical of the animal that the old bear that so scared Kerfoot when he was focussing his camera upon her should have simply sat down on her haunches and stared open-eyed at us when we rolled on the ground in laughter.

Nor is this kind of bluff and this attitude toward failure to make good on the part of the Black Bear, confined to intercourse with strangers. I have seen one of them go through exactly similar actions with another bear. One of the most amusing little incidents I ever watched—because it so laughably illustrated the happy-go-lucky, anything-to-keep-one's-self-amused attitude of these beasts—will serve as an example. I had been watching a Black Bear that was feeding in ignorance of my presence, and after some time it had sat down at the foot of a small pine tree on a side hill and was leaning lazily against the trunk, turning its head now and then as though watching for something to turn up. It was a pretty good-sized bear—three hundred pounds or so perhaps—and when another animal of about its own size appeared some distance along the side hill and, somewhat to my surprise, began to walk threateningly toward it, I became very much interested. The first bear, however, did not seem to share my interest. He paid, or pretended to pay, no attention whatever to the newcomer. And the latter, very deliberate but very determined, came straight toward him. When he arrived at the other side of the small tree (it was not more than six inches thick) he half drew back on his haunches, half raised his fore-quarters from the ground, lifted one paw as if to strike, and uttered the coughing snarl ending in a rapid champing of the jaws that is the Black Bear's ultimate expression of wrath. I thought that I was going to have a reserved seat at a prize fight. But my original bear continued to lean against his tree and look about lazily as though waiting for something interesting to turn up. He did not seem to so much as suspect that there was another bear in that neck of the woods. And the challenger turned round and walked away as deliberate, as dignified, and as unconcerned as though nothing whatever had happened.

The actions of these two bears, moreover, illustrate another characteristic of the tribe. You never watch Black Bear when they are quite at home and undisturbed without being made to feel that they are hard put to it to know what to do with themselves. A grizzly "knows his business" in every sense of the expression. When he starts out, he knows where is he going and goes there. When he starts a job, he finishes it and goes on to the next. I have followed one along and over the high ridges of the Rockies for two days on end when the light snow of early fall showed every step he took. I have tracked one from ground-squirrel burrow to marmot hole; seen where two hours of incredibly laborious digging had yielded him a mouthful of breakfast; followed his careful search for more provender, to be got by more digging, and seen where, the possibilities of that particular ridge having been exhausted, he had started on a predetermined journey across country for another feeding ground. The grizzly is *working for his living* and knows it.

But Black Bear act for all the world like boys on a rainy Saturday. They've got nothing but time, and the one problem in life is how to kill it. Watch one for a couple of hours and you'll see him start forty different things, finish none of them, and then sit down and swing his head hopelessly from side to side as though to say, "Now *what* shall I do next?"

If you have only seen these animals in captivity you are apt to think that their air of restless boredom is due to their confinement; that they don't know what to do with themselves because they are unable, in a bear pit, to follow their natural vocations. I am always sorry for wild animals in captivity, but I am, I think, less sorry for the Black Bear than for most others. For they act just about as bored to death in the woods as they do in the Zoo. I have seen one come along, rip a piece off an old stump, sniff for bugs, find none, stand undecided for a few minutes, and then walk up to a tree and draw itself upright against the trunk, stretching like a cat. It then sat down at the foot of the tree and scratched its ear. It then got up and started off aimlessly, but, happening to straddle a low bush in its path and liking the feeling of the branches against its belly, it walked backward and forward half a dozen times to repeat the sensation. Then it started back the way it had come and smelling a mouse under a log, suddenly woke up and became all attention. It tried to move the log and failed. It dug a bit at one end but gave that up. It then tried again, very hard this time, to turn the log over, and the log giving away suddenly, the bear turned a complete somersault backward, but instantly recovered itself and rushed around with the most ludicrous haste to see if the mouse had gotten away. It hadn't. It hadn't had time. Which may give you a faint notion of how quick that clumsy-looking bear was when he really got awake. After he had eaten the mouse he was up against it again. He didn't know what to do next. There was a fallen tree near by and he got up on the trunk and walked the length of it. Then he turned around (quite hard to do without touching the ground, but he was very careful) and walked back again to the butt. Here he stood and looked straight ahead of him—stood at gaze, as the old romancers used to say. Then (the log was perhaps eighteen inches high) he climbed down backward very slowly and carefully as if he were afraid of falling, and walked around to examine a place where the upturned roots had left a hole in the earth. Finally he sat down and began "weaving." That is to say, he began swinging his head from side to side, making a figure ∞ with his nose, as one often sees them do behind the bars of the Zoo. There is nothing in the world more expressive of hopeless ennui.

But although one is constantly tempted to call the Black Bear names; to refer to him as an idle, pottering, purposeless, "footless," lazy, loafing tramp; he can upon occasion be the most persistent thing on four feet (always excepting a porcupine), and the fact that he has no business of his own to attend to by no means deters him from poking his sharp nose into any and everything that doesn't concern him. There never was a more convincing example of the fact that idle hands (and paws) are supplied by Satan with mischievous occupation. He is chock-full of inquisitiveness and eaten up with curiosity. And if you imagine that because he's clumsy he can't be quick, or that because he acts foolish he is anybody's fool, you will be very far out of the right reckoning.

One Black Bear in one-half hour can do more to

make an unguarded camp look like a hurrah's nest than any other known agency; and I have had one come back half a dozen times from half a dozen different directions, to try to get at my camera to paw it over and find out what it was. One day when I was photographing grizzlies I buried the tin case that held my electric battery while I went back to camp for something. I did this because I knew that there were Black Bear in the neighborhood, and I hoped by this trick to keep them from tampering with my effects. But when I got back a Black Bear had been there, had dug up the case, pulled the cover off, chewed the tin all out of shape, and had bitten holes in each of the dry batteries. Another time I found one sitting under a canvas shoulder bag that I had hung on the branch of a tree, hitting it first with one paw and then with another as it swung. He made so comical a picture that I watched him for a while, but when he reached out his snout and grasped the bag with his teeth I hurriedly drove him away, for the bag had some wooden cylinders of flash powder in it.

On the trip when Mr. Kerfoot and I were working together we frequently built ourselves seats in convenient trees from which to watch for grizzlies, and operated the electric mechanisms of our cameras by strings stretched from the apparatus to our crannies among the branches. On one occasion, when we determined to work a second night from the same location, we left these strings in position so as to save ourselves the considerable trouble of running them a second time. But the next night when we came to set up our cameras we could not find the ends of the strings. There had been two of them running to widely separated points, each one hundred feet or so distant from our look-out. And we could find neither of them. Finally, I climbed to the seat in the tree to see if I could find the other ends of the string, and discovered that a Black Bear during our absence had been trying our seat, and had pulled both strings in and left them hopelessly snarled up among the branches. He had, I suppose, found our scent on the tree, followed it up to investigate, found the seat (a piece of board nailed across two limbs), and having his curiosity aroused by the strings, had pulled them in to see what was at the other end.

There was a fairly well-trodden bear trail that led under this same tree, and that night, after we had got things shipshape again, we had another amusing object lesson in the ways of the Black Bear. We had little more than got settled for our long wait for dusk and the coming of the grizzlies, when we saw a lean old Black Bear with one cub coming down the trail toward our tree. When they got within thirty feet or so of us the mother stopped, evidently seeing us. But the cub kept on. Whereupon the mother called it back and it sat down beside her. Then began one of the most farcical exhibitions I ever saw. This old bear (Kerfoot declared her to be an old maid that had married late in life) was evidently used to going down that particular trail and wasn't going to change her habits on account of any interlopers. But at the same time she was afraid to pass the tree with us in it. She would come on a few steps and then back off again. Then she would wander up and down in the most undecided and worried way, grumbling and growling to herself. Finally she sat down and fairly cried—moaning and whining like a spoiled child. All the while the cub kept running ahead and then turning round to look back, as much as to say, "Come on, it's all right. What's the matter with you to-night?" And, of course, all the time the whole Rocky Mountains was open to her to go round by. Once she went back the way she came and we thought we were rid of her. But she came back again and recommenced the performance. Then I got down and drove her off.

Black Bear are found pretty generally in grizzly countries except in places where the grizzlies are very plenty, and now that they are all scarce they cover the same ranges almost everywhere. In the early nineties, in the Selkirks in British Columbia, I never saw a Black Bear. Now, however, although the grizzlies are still as plentiful there as anywhere, the Black Bear are numerous. But the Black fellows are mighty careful never to get in the grizzlies' way. I have seen one stand up on his hind legs behind the trunk of a good-sized tree and sidle round it, peeking out as he went to watch a grizzly bear go by; and I have already told how the two Black Bear took to the trees when they heard a grizzly coming. I know of nothing that better illustrates the keen senses of these animals than the way in which they will detect the approach of a grizzly long before a man's senses can make him aware of the fact. In the Yellowstone National Park, where there are many animals of both species occupying the same ranges, I found that I could always get warning of the approach of the grizzlies when their twilight feeding time approached by the sudden and complete disappearance of the Black Bear; and on several occasions, in different parts of the mountains, when the frequent flashes of our electric cameras had scared the grizzlies away from that part of the wood, the Black Bear seemed, strangely enough, to be aware of the fact and made no attempt to retire at their usual hour. This was so interesting an exhibition of keen senses or quick intuition that I watched very carefully during the whole period of my stay to try to satisfy myself as to the source of their knowledge. The fact that they began to be uneasy as the usual hour for the grizzlies' arrival came near, sometimes led me to think that they merely judged from past experience as to how long it was safe for them to stay out. But, on the other hand, I saw so many cases where a sudden suspicion of unexpected danger led them to make themselves scarce, and this, too, when the suspicion turned out to have been right, that I was forced to conclude that they either heard or smelled their enemies. But I could never find out which it was that they did. Several times I have seen them suddenly rush with snorts of apprehension to the nearest tree, and had their actions explained a few minutes later by the silent appearance of a huge grizzly.

The grandest wild animal of the United States is the grizzly bear. But the most amusing the most ludicrous, the most human and understandable of our wild animals, is our friend *Ursus americanus* (Pallas). I have called him the Happy Hooligan of the woods, and I can think of no more descriptive phrase for him. He is neither evil-intentioned nor bad-natured. Yet he has probably terrified more innocent wayfarers than any other denizen of our forests.

THE GRIZZLY BEAR

Charles Scribner's Sons, New York